Tainted Love

God, Sex & Relationships for
the Not-So-Pure-at-Heart

David Mark Brown

InterVarsity Press
Downers Grove, Illinois

InterVarsity Press
P.O. Box 1400, Downers Grove, IL 60515-1426
World Wide Web: www.ivpress.com
E-mail: mail@ivpress.com

InterVarsity Press® is the book-publishing division of InterVarsity Christian Fellowship/ USA®, a student movement active on campus at hundreds of universities, colleges and schools of nursing in the United States of America, and a member movement of the International Fellowship of Evangelical Students. For information about local and regional activities, write Public Relations Dept., InterVarsity Christian Fellowship/USA, 6400 Schroeder Rd., P.O. Box 7895, Madison, WI 53707-7895, or visit the IVCF website at <www.ivcf.org>.

Scripture quotations, unless otherwise noted, are from the New Revised Standard Version of the Bible, copyright 1989 by the Division of Christian Education of the National Council of the Churches of Christ in the USA. Used by permission. All rights reserved.

Cover photograph: © Bill Sykes Images/Photonica

ISBN 0-8308-2324-7

Printed in the United States of America ∞

Library of Congress Cataloging-in-Publication Data

Brown, David Mark, 1974-
  Tainted love: god, sex & relationships for the not-so-pure-at-heart/
David Mark Brown.
    p. cm.
Includes bibliographical references (p.   )
  ISGN 0-8308-2324-7
  1. Christian life—Meditations. 2. Love—Religious
aspects—Christianity. 3. Body, Human—Religious aspects—Christianity.
4. Sex—Religious aspects—Christianity. I. Title.

BV4501.3 .B76 2002
  241',66—dc21
                                                              2002004054

| P | 15 | 14 | 13 | 12 | 11 | 10 | 9 | 8 | 7 | 6 | 5 | 4 | 3 | 2 | 1 |
| Y | 13 | 12 | 11 | 10 | 09 | 08 | 07 | 06 | 05 | 04 | 03 | 02 | | | |

I began writing this book six months into an eighteen-month engagement to the love of my (so far) short life. She, along with my roommate, has challenged and taught me much. These two have had special access—whether blessed or cursed—to almost every moment of my college life. They continue to have great influence on the thoughts in this book. I dedicate this book to them and to Jesus my Lord, who suffers through all of my failures and rejoices with all of my successes.

Contents

Preface

Once during a gentle but heavy snow I sat on a rock outcropping that over-looked the Missoula valley. The sound-absorbing silence of nightfall and snow crushed in on my noisy soul. I had been so loud, so dizzying in my attempt to perform the Christian life out of my abilities. Finally in tears I uttered, "It's all you. It's all you, Jesus." Suddenly all the noise and crush became silence. My heart, light as the flakes falling around me, for a moment experienced God's beauty. His perfect will reigned in me.

Possibly the only way to understand what I mean by "God's beauty" is to recall those fleeting moments when everything seemed to fit together and make sense. Maybe such a moment came for you as a display of lightning shocked you with the vastness of the gap between God and humans. Maybe it came as you witnessed a birth or a death. Maybe it came in an answer to a crisis of faith.

It is in these moments we feel pure and good and whole. But most of the time our feelings are entirely the opposite of pure. This book is about how we pursue purity through the discovery of beauty: God's beauty in us and in others.

This is a book for those who hope to be more Christlike and those who have given up hope, who fear that reading this will only pile on more guilt over evil thoughts and deeds. I am writing for those tempted to surrender faith in exchange for numbness, or to escape a feeling of judgment. I am writing for anyone who has tried to love with purity and found that it was tainted by sin.

This book is not for those who are doing a good job at being a Christian or whose small sins are under control. My sins are wild and flagrant. They ride me, deride me and challenge me to hide them. I cannot. They rule a part of my life. I write to expose them. I write in hopes that we can all share our struggles with sin and perversion, thus allowing Jesus to rule over the sin as well as the sinner.

Exposed

Recently I got a rare opportunity to expose my wretched self to a crowd. The experience was bizarre but freeing. Our campus was visited by an open-air damnation preacher. You know the kind—let's call him Brother G. He was ranting about horny little frat boys, whores and queers. Everyone that came by was threatened with burning in hell. The first time I walked by he pointed and projected loudly, "There goes a horny little devil."

I felt offended. I felt embarrassed a bit. Mostly I felt angry that someone was so loudly proclaiming my God in a way that was so far from my understanding of him. But I was late for an appointment, so I kept on my quiet way. After my appointment I came back by the place where Brother G had been speaking. Some security folk were talking with him while a small crowd lingered on the patio. I asked someone what had happened; a young lady had flown out of the crowd and unleashed a dizzying assault on Brother G.

I waited for the crowd to dissipate, then I approached Brother G. I wanted to talk civilly to the man for a bit; unfortunately I heard everything I expected. He believed he had won victory over sin, and God had called him to direct others to the same perfection. I discussed my disagreement with his views and how he was relating them to others. As we parted ways he informed me that he would be speaking again the next day at the same time.

I have experienced deep grief over this kind of perfectionist doctrine, and the last thing I wanted was for others to experience the apparently heavy hand of God. The next day, as Brother G began to assault passersby, I started to ask him questions. People stopped to listen, and a crowd formed again. After a short while our conversation revealed that Brother G believed himself to be perfect. At this people scoffed. He asked me if I sinned. "Yes," I replied loudly. He asked me if I ever viewed pornography. I replied once again with a loud yes. He asked me if I masturbated to that pornography. I replied, sadly but truthfully, "Yes."

Brother G thought he had won a convincing victory. He spouted about how I claimed to be a minister and a spiritual guide and yet was a pervert. I do not remember what I said next as much as I remember the emotion surrounding the experience. I was both one of God's children and one of the crowd. Whereas Brother G claimed to stand apart, I claimed to stand with the crowd in the struggle with sin.

Many people, Christian and non-Christian alike, came up to thank me afterward. The experience gave them new eyes through which to see Christians and Christianity. The experience also gave me new eyes through which to see my perverted nature. I was no longer an island of lust and lechery; I was a wave being tossed in an ocean of sinful and hurting people. In my sin I belonged to the crowd, to all humankind.

This book is for everyone in the crowd, tossed about in the ocean of sin.

Chapter One

The Battle for Purity

The lighting is dim. The last rays of sunset still frustrate the TV screen with their glare. The day has been long; I welcome the time alone to watch a romantic comedy. An abundant array of beverages promises to keep me quenched for 144 minutes of movie pleasure. My chair reclines to the perfect angle, and I place my afghan, a gift from my grandmother, across my legs. Grasping the remote as a king would grasp a sword, I press Play.

I love movies. I grew strong on *Star Wars* and *Raiders of the Lost Ark.* I grew up and then down some with *The Outsiders, The Fugitive* and *Animal House.* I dreamed with *Groundhog Day, Sleepless in Seattle* and *Ever After.* I stepped out with *Joe Versus the Volcano* and *Braveheart.* I hurt with *Return to Me, Say Anything* and *The Breakfast Club.* I found peaceful sleep with *Beauty and the Beast* and *The Princess Bride.* I laughed with *So I Married an Axe Murderer, The Waterboy, Ace Ventura* and *Raising Arizona.* I marveled at *The Matrix, 2001: A Space Odyssey* and *Twelve Monkeys.*

I live in a world populated by people with beliefs different from mine. Often I suspend my values when I push off into the deeps of a cinematic adventure. I could not have possibly known the content of every scene in this movie; by loading it into the player I have signed an invisible contract to observe and appreciate every shot for its artistic potential. The couple brushes close and sways toward the bedroom, and I remind myself to appreciate their love and God's visible genius in creating man and woman—

specifically, *this* particularly photogenic woman.

She *is* beautiful; that is not evil. I can widen my eyes over her for the length of the movie moment. Of course I dare not rewind or, God forbid, use the freeze frame. That would be too much. That would be immoral.

I am glad to be watching this movie alone.

My heart rides the tides of the movie. As the credits scroll up the screen I realize that I have been changed. I am happy, even excited about love and life. But *my* world seems dim. Will my world ever be like *theirs?* Or should it? Which world will guide my next actions?

Not Pure at Heart

I am not pure at heart. I am in the deepest way a pervert.

The word *pervert* grates our ears and carries many connotations with it. It shrieks like Howard Stern's voice over the radio or Howard Hughes's fingernails on a thirteen story chalkboard. But I do not apologize for my use of the word; it is the right word for my meaning. It has been appropriate since the Fall of humankind.

I clearly remember my InterVarsity Christian Fellowship staff orientation in Madison, Wisconsin. I was beaming to see the "Graceland" of the Inter-Varsity movement, and I chanted softly to myself on the plane, "I'm going to Graceland, Graceland—Madison, Wisconsin."

In addition to InterVarsity, Madison is home to a wild and liberal college culture. We submerged ourselves into that environment. Don't get me wrong; we prayed and studied Scripture like all good ministers do, but we also wandered the streets in search of conversations, looking for God in the midst of some pretty whacked-out stuff.

A small band of us, feeling adventurous, wandered into an alternative-lifestyle clothing/gift shop. We shrugged our shoulders and smiled politely at bumper stickers about bongs and aliens and politics. At other slogans we stopped smiling altogether.

Then I noticed a T-shirt that immediately fascinated me. It was a simple white shirt with a colored collar and bands around the bottom of the sleeves. It was sized strictly for women and made to be worn tight. Written in bold across the chest was the word: "PERVERT." I smiled despite myself, wishing that the shirt were available in men's sizes. The statement was simple and true, one of the truest I think anyone can make.

We have all gone down that road. We could all honestly wear that shirt. While everything that God has created in me and given to me is good, I pervert it all. So I use the word *pervert* not to describe child molesters or any particular sinner but to describe all of us, who have all fallen short of God's pure design.

A Dictionary Definition of Perversion
A deviation from what is considered right or good; obstinate disobedience.

I am not pure at heart. I do not believe that any of us is. We are all perverted images of what God designed us to be. Ecclesiastes 7:29 puts it this way: "See, this alone I found, that God made human beings straightforward, but they have devised many schemes."

Our Definition of Perversion
Anything short of purity; anything deviant from God; everything since the Garden of Eden—except for Jesus. Jesus is right and good.

The Bible instructs us to be perfect, without sin (1 John 3:2-6), and yet tells us that we cannot be without sin during this life (1 John 1:8-10). Somehow we live under the conditions of both of these statements. This conflict between perfection and perversion—being a sinner and a child of God—drives us crazy, brings us to our knees, compels us to shake our fists, lifts us high in praise and drops us low in desperation.

During my freshman year at the University of Montana I earned the nickname "H." A friend who lived across the hall watched me carry my Bible almost everywhere—even into the bathroom stalls. At the same time he observed that my roommate and I had stolen one of the study lounge sofas. We kept it in our dorm room, covered by a large blanket. Within a few weeks everyone on our floor knew me as "Heathen," which thankfully was later shortened to "H."

We desire and strive to be perfect, but alas, we thwart our own cause.

And still God resides in us and reaches out to us. Our search for perfection leads us outside ourselves. As we recognize and respond to God's beauty in us and in the rest of his creation, God brings us closer to his beautiful design.

> Why do you submit to regulations, "Do not handle, Do not taste, Do not touch"? All these regulations refer to things that perish with use; they are simply human commands and teachings. These have indeed an appearance of wisdom in promoting self-imposed piety, humility, and severe treatment of the body, but they are of no value in checking self-indulgence. (Colossians 2:20-23)

As perverts we cannot purify ourselves in God's sight, and we must never confuse striving for purity with being good or pleasing to God. Our quest for purity is about understanding God and relating to him, not pleasing him. God has his own reasons for finding pleasure in us.

A Dictionary Definition of Purity *Freedom from anything that adulterates or taints; a state of being unmixed, faultless, blameless.*

Our Definition of Purity *Purity of what? Purity is not meant to stand alone. Read purity as pure beauty, a synonym for perfection.*

The Spectrum of Beauty

God created the world up to his standards. His beauty is in everything he makes. Everything known to us has been created by God; therefore everything on earth is beautiful. But we take the things God made beautiful and we pervert them. Through this intermingling of God's beautiful creation and our acts of perversion we have a spectrum of God's beauty that resembles the spectrum of light.

Light overcomes darkness. Darkness is nothing more than the absence of light. Therefore, darkness exposed to light ceases to be darkness, while the light does not cease to be light. The same is true for God's beauty. If you expose perversion to beauty, the perversion becomes beauty. God's beauty overcomes perversion.

Compare the human heart—human being—to a room. The room was designed to be well-lit, but suppose that someone has drawn the shades and turned off all the lights. We can barely make out the shape and contents of the room, but the fact that we can see even that little of the room indicates that light is still present. And the room gets lighter and brighter with each new bulb lit into it, with each curtain opened. As more light enters the room, fewer dark places remain. Even if we hide in one dark corner of the room and cover ourselves with blankets to shade the light, even if we snuff out all but one light bulb, the room is still lit.

According to Genesis 1:27, humankind was created in God's image. If God is ultimate beauty and humans are images of that beauty, nothing we do can remove the image in which we were created. He and his beauty are infinite. Even if only a small trace of God's beauty still exists in our hearts, we are still beautiful. This is how God's beauty works.

God's beauty has been, is being and will be played out in the world all around us. We have witnessed the stuff of his creation. We have viewed the movie of God's grace. We have seen the passion play, with its climax unfolding on the cross. The credits have been rolling ever since. This is the precious moment. Which world do we let dictate our reality? Ours—at best a perverted beauty denying the presence of pure beauty and offering short-lived happiness, shallow contentment, hurt, failure and shame—or God's?

A Dictionary Definition of Beauty
The quality of being very pleasing, as in form, color, etc.

Our Definition of Beauty
Anything of God. Anything that reflects God, even dimly, has beauty in it. Pure beauty is therefore anything that reflects God perfectly.

Chapter Two

Why Am I Drawn to Sin?
A Foundation for Perversion

The black and quiet buzz is swallowed by the opening shot—a blurry, broad-brushed pan from left to right across lively green and pushy blue patches. Gentle strokes of music begin. Strings and wordless vocals weave the fabric on a warp of messaging bass hits. Sounds of nature speak the chorus and the verses. The picture zooms in and slows down, finally focusing on a caterpillar crawling across rich soil. A hand reaches down to provide for the caterpillar a free ride to a shining leaf, for the viewer a scale of the imagery. The shot widens, moving along the arm, gradually revealing uncovered Man—unapologizing, unashamed Man. He shines as if the dew treats him like every other part of creation. He would not be handsome if it were not for his ease. Nothing about him is rough or exaggerated. Nothing about him speaks of arrogance or pride, weakness or fear.

Something in you realizes he is beautiful, but you hesitate, half ashamed and half curious.

This scene from God's movie demonstrates his authority and power, but it also displays his sensuality and sense of beauty. God shaped the raindrop. He shaped the human body, the leaf, the killer whale and the double helix. God creates beauty.

The man treads unburdened soil with near weightlessness. He follows no trail, but he takes each step with confidence—not so much as if he knows where he is going, but as if he has no need to know. You cheer for him already, but you are afraid.

We Are Divided

We are divided people. We remember our Creator, and we recall security and peace, beauty and simple appreciation: gratitude. We sit in a car on an unhurried, rainy evening, and we listen to jazz until the battery starts to run low. During a lightning storm we applaud the strobe-lit sky. We eat five fluffy peach-filled pastries lovingly made by an old lady who speaks with a foreign tongue. We leave our work inside and join neighbor kids in a sprinkler without even changing clothes. We interrupt a late-night drive and lie on the warm hood of our car, looking beyond other planets into shining stars. We put aside sleep to sit with a hurting friend. In these moments we are closest to God, clinging to a trace of our original image of God's beauty.

In a wonderfully wise children's book titled *The Little Prince,* the main character finds himself in the Sahara Desert far from his home planet but In the presence of the narrator, who has become a dear friend during their brief sojourn.

> "Men," said the little prince, "set out on their way in express trains, but they do not know what they are looking for. Then they rush about, and get excited, and turn round and round. . . . It is not worth the trouble. . . .
>
> "The men where you live," said the little prince, "raise five thousand roses in the same garden—and they do not find in it what they are looking for. . . . And yet, what they are looking for could be found in one single rose, or in a little water. . . .
>
> "But the eyes are blind. One must look with the heart."[*]

God's image in us alerts us, warms us, awakens us to beauty. But each one of us, out of morbid curiosity, neglects the beauty and seeks out the shadows.

In the shadows we get angry at traffic. We covet neighbors' toys. We envy

---

[*]Antoine de Saint-Exupéry, *The Little Prince* (New York: Harcourt Brace Jovanovich, 1971), pp. 94-97.

friends' successes. We lust after desirable women or men on TV. We steal from, cheat on, lie to and hurt those closest to us because they no longer satisfy us. We abuse ourselves because we are not as good as someone else.

But we are not solely children of the shadows. Even when we feel worthless and evil, we are still children of God—children of light. The apostle Paul describes this state in detail:

> So I find it to be a law that when I want to do what is good, evil lies close at hand. For I delight in the law of God in my inmost self, but I see in my members another law at war with the law of my mind, making me captive to the law of sin that dwells in my members. Wretched man that I am! Who will rescue me from this body of death? Thanks be to God through Jesus Christ our Lord!
>
> So then, with my mind I am a slave to the law of God, but with my flesh I am a slave to the law of sin. (Romans 7:21-25)

Above the Crowd

This is how we see ourselves,
unfocused and yet unyielding.
This is how we share ourselves,
spread malcontent like spores
on whispery winds from willowy spirits:
(Oh hollow heart resonate until your tone resounds in every vessel.)

My pain spills over in drops of sweat
falling from my brow in rhythm with the pounding
of my feet falling, my shins splinting
and the pavement calling: forget
forget, forget. I cannot. You made my body
ugly. I still burn though my muscles are strong.

My pain spills over in acid and bile
and alcohol of happy youth.

My parents loved me here
to this toilette. Love me now as I heave
your conditions and disappointments into this swirling bowl
and open my mouth again to swallow respite.

My pain spills over in tears and laughter
with tales I tell of hell and
my residence there. I laugh
now my loved ones are gone
and no one comes near. I am a sinner,
but I have paid my dues and hid my tears.

I brag hollow tones
beating my heart's drum—
I am more self-destructive than you,
I have been degraded beyond pity
into humor, but not humility.
This is the excrement that is me which
I grab in my palms, squeeze in my fists
and shove into my stomach again.

My pain spills over in the movement of my bowels
expelling, expressing all that I am
the only way I know how.
That is to say, with the arrogance of my lips
I hold my excrement above the crowd and shout
this is the only remarkable thing about me.

Many scoff at suggestions for finding a pure lifestyle. Some have tried
everything short of throwing faith away. Even as I write this I know that I am
no nearer to living a life full of pure deeds and decisions than I was two years
ago, four years ago or more.

But striving for purity is not about being good. Striving for purity is about knowing God. My failures over the years have produced an awe in me. I am amazed that God has not struck me dead. I am amazed that he claims his love is for even me. As much as I hope to choose more consistently against sin and perversion, I know that I have not defeated sin. But in the wake of sin I can see more clearly his perfect beauty and the distortion my sin causes. My struggle for purity has led me to know my God better.

Child of the Shadows?

How can we be evil and still be pure? How can I be a child of God when my actions seem to be controlled by the devil? I have asked myself these questions and have heard them asked by many others. As we mature in the Christian faith we find that certain sin behaviors do not leave us. At the same time our expectations rise greatly. We hold higher standards for ourselves, and yet we are still capable of the same sin year after year.

We get the horrible sense that we have failed at Christianity, that we are children of the shadows—bad people pretending to be good. We decide that the image of God in us is an illusion, and we believe the excrement of our lives to be our defining characteristics. We boast of the shadows as if it's all we can claim as our own ("I got so drunk last night").

We are perverted, but we are not children of perversion. No matter how disgusted we are with ourselves, we have been created in the image of God and purchased by Jesus to be his brothers and sisters. Romans 3:23 puts it this way: "All have sinned and fall short of the glory of God; they are now justified by his grace as a gift, through the redemption that is in Christ Jesus." Recognizing our perversion is an important step, but it is not our final step. We must cling defiantly to God until our wretchedness reveals God's beauty.

What Is Our Response?

Uncovered humanity is beautiful, but we hesitate to look, half ashamed and half curious. For some reason we are not comfortable with nakedness. What do we do with it?

We can choose to close our eyes tight. There are times when it is appropriate to surround ourselves with Christian community and shield ourselves from risky encounters. But we must not adopt sheltered growth as a permanent lifestyle. Those who do run their own risks; they risk outward righteousness but internal emotional stuntedness. They may find it difficult to make and keep good friends. They may feel lonely even as they feel superior. They may wear themselves out developing elaborate plans to protect themselves from themselves, with strict and detailed rules about entertainment, companionship and other lifestyle issues, creating a complicated maze of barriers to close relationships.

I recently saw a small-town production of *Camelot.* Lance (Sir Lancelot), who held purity quite highly, maintained a strict regimen that allowed indulgence in nothing impure. Then he met Jenny (Lady Guinevere), the wife of his king, Arthur. Despite (and maybe because of) all his rules and harsh disciplines, Lance fell for Jenny, caused the downfall of Camelot and broke apart his friendship with Arthur and Jenny.

Lance held strict rules of purity, and still they were not enough to make him pure of heart. In fact, his strict rules and lack of experience in appreciating beauty may have even played a part in his betrayal of himself and those he loved. Closing our eyes to beauty leaves us empty and ignorant, and still we are not safe.

Closing our eyes to beauty leaves us empty and ignorant, and still we are not safe.

The second response is common enough to this generation: we open ourselves wide to everything we see. We sample life indiscriminately, throwing away boundaries and guidelines, and making the simplistic assumption that God will protect us from hurt.

Those who make this choice often become emotionally calloused or confused. They may find loyalty and commitment difficult. They may become adrenaline junkies always needing a higher degree of stimulus, becoming bored with things that once held great pleasure. In their search for beauty they prohibit nothing, and soon everything becomes dull.

But this is not the first time God has watched his creation overindulge. King Solomon knew very well the struggle that grips us today.

I said to myself, "Come now, I will make a test of pleasure; enjoy yourself." But again, this also was vanity. . . . Whatever my eyes desired I did not keep from them; I kept my heart from no pleasure, for my heart found pleasure in all my toil, and this was my reward for all my toil. Then I considered all that my hands had done and the toil I had spent in doing it, and again, all was vanity and a chasing after wind, and there was nothing to be gained under the sun. (Ecclesiastes 2:1, 10-11)

So which will it be? Do we look away and shield our eyes from the beauty around us? Do we open our eyes wide, take in and chase after everything we can see, and leave it to God to keep us from sin? Are there other options?

Chapter Three

Rediscovering the Source of Purity & Perversion

The two stand there together, swallowed in discovery. To any human, discovery is the first beauty. Adam stretches his forehead and cheeks to open his eyes wider. Then he focuses with flashing scrutiny before breaking into complete awe and wonder. There is a certain fear, of the same brand he has for his Creator, when he focuses on their differences. Some obvious, some gentle, he takes time to notice them all—as much as his senses can tell him.

But it is their similarities that surprise him more. These he noticed first, and he soon returns to them. Every other creature is quite different, almost totally different now that Eve is here.

Eve's Gift (for Keri)

Human skin wrapped warm around bundles,
glands, muscles, nerves, and blood—
tiny fiber-ways weaving blue and red
hidden below the curving surface pumping and then quiet,
pumping and then quiet—form this woman.
A lofty visionary with work-worn hands uncalloused
turned gold into flesh with his touch,
and saw the beauty of a river bank curved by rushing water,
a water drop—the natural shape of motion and breath.

She holds this energy
this grace quietly, a constant caterpillar.
People pin butterflies to their belt.
People hunt butterflies and pin then up
and gawk at them dripping comments about beauty.
Afraid to be hunted, afraid not to be found
"It is safest" to be cocooned in shame, not to be proud
of her strength and wear it boldly on her chest.

I told her a story about two naked people.
He held his hand just above her skin
all over, over every inch with shock and joy
sparking the air between his fingers and every hair
every freckle every chill bump of her body.
Her entire spirit spoke through those fine
profound differences and moved his hand
demanding and giving respect, offering
him the courage he must have
within her wings.

Here we are: God's beauty. Naked, selfless, giving, innocent, pure of heart—we walk in the garden with our Creator. We are not exploiting native peoples, growing herbal narcotics or soliciting immoral favors. We have an unblemished spiritual, emotional and physical relationship.

This is what we had to lose. This is also what we have to regain.

The Original Perversion

The first perversion was the act of perverting beauty. Service was forsaken for self-service. Eve tasted the fruit of a forbidden tree because she saw that the tree was "good for food," "a delight to the eyes" and "to be desired to make one wise" (Genesis 3:6). Adam happily joined in. They served themselves rather than their God. What they had been given was not enough; the beauty around them was not beautiful enough.

Their stumbling is our stumbling. We lose faith in God's good provision for a certain area of our lives—providing a spouse, caring for our sense of belonging, taking away a repetitive sin. We allow ourselves to be convinced that God is holding out on us, and our needs and desires can be better fulfilled under our own management. We suspect that satisfaction lurks out there and God would withhold it from us. And in our attempt to feed ourselves, we slap away the hand that has the only lasting food. This begins our alienation from God and our perversion of the beauty he placed in us and created for us.

Bricks in a Wall

Eve and Adam built a wall between them and God, brick by brick. This was their wall, not God's. But all too often it is our wall as well.

Pride. Adam and Eve decided they knew better than God. They put their own logic before God's clear and direct command. Pride is not often obvious, but it undergirds every other brick in the walls we build.

Doubt. They wondered if God really had their best interests in mind. They doubted that he was totally good. They doubted his commitment to serving them. Doubt cannot create a wall between God and us on its own; it is a hollow brick—easily tossed around. It is never certain of anything, even itself, so it is very unstable. But doubt is cheap and easy, and so it combines with other bricks to make a very effective wall.

Greed. Adam and Eve had at their fingertips every other tree in the garden. They had all they could ever need. They had each other and a perfect relationship with God. They had peace, security, comfort and love. They decided to surrender their contentment to greed, and they forfeited it all. Greed is an ugly and ostentatious brick, quickly made and quickly laid in an urgent lust for more bricks and a higher wall.

Fear. Adam and Eve were afraid to let God maintain a monopoly on the knowledge of good and evil. They were afraid to be seen completely naked in his presence (Genesis 3:10). No matter which way you stack the bricks, Adam and Eve were afraid. Fear is the mortar between the bricks. Our wall is founded on pride but held together by fear.

Shame and guilt. When Adam and Eve's "eyes were opened," they were shocked. They were attacked with shame and guilt when they became aware of the disgusting wall they had carelessly thrown together. They were now *ashamed* to be naked, so they continued to build the wall. "Build it higher so God cannot even see us!" Shame is defined in part as dishonor or disgrace. In their shame Adam and Eve lost favor and honor—they were *disgraced*—in each other's eyes. But God did not say to them, "You ought to be ashamed."

Guilt differs slightly from shame. Adam and Eve hid from God out of guilt over their betrayal of him. While their shame was directed toward their newfound perversion, their guilt was directed toward their actions, which left them perverted, sloppily adorned with fig leaves and clumsily hidden from God behind bark and fruit (which had gotten them into trouble in the first

---

Deconstructing the Wall

1. *What in your life do you see as "the sin"? What perversion rises to the surface first during moments when you hate who you are?*

2. *With this sin in mind, consider how the different bricks in the wall (pride, doubt, greed, fear, shame, guilt) play a part in separating you from God. Do you fear God's judgment? Does your pride put you in place of God as the provider for your needs? Does greed sabotage your contentment? Be specific.*

3. *Read the apostle Paul's take on perversion from Romans 7:18—8:2, 31-39. Your wall may still be standing. You may still be building it, but no wall—no fortress of sin—no matter how massive, can separate you from the love of Christ. Can you believe this? What will it take for you to trust Christ's love?*

4. *Share this exercise honestly with God and a trustworthy friend. Make sure that both you and your friend understand and respect the level of intimacy involved.*

---

place). The bricks of guilt are laid slowly, sometimes long after the main wall has been built. They can even replace crumbling and faulty bricks to keep the wall from tumbling down.

Shame and guilt are unique in that they are often given to you by others who sin against you, but ultimately it is your hand that places them on your wall.

Inevitable Victory in the Face of Insurmountable Odds

The Garden of Eden, as we have read about it, is gone forever. But if we left off there, what would be the purpose of this book? Adam and Eve were created, sinned and died. We, on the other hand, are still alive. We have also sinned, but can we change our course before we go the way of our ancestors? Can we stop being perverts? Can we live a pure life?

We need to be close to God, but we run into a problem: God can't be close to something so screwed up. And we have proven over and over through our many failures that we can't purify ourselves.

What can we do? Well, the reign of perversion on earth was broken up by God sending his Son, Jesus Christ. Through Jesus we can come close to God again.

> There is therefore now no condemnation for those who are in Christ Jesus. For the law of the Spirit of life in Christ Jesus has set you free from the law of sin and of death. For God has done what the law, weakened by the flesh, could not do: by sending his own Son in the likeness of sinful flesh, and to deal with sin, he condemned sin in the flesh, so that the just requirement of the law might be fulfilled in us, who walk not according to the flesh but according to the Spirit. (Romans 8:1-4)

We are not condemned. We are justified. The sin that we are bound by and powerless to overcome can be lifted off of us by Jesus Christ. We can be free. In Christ we are already free.

But we must play an active role. We must change our focus from the world to God. We must break our stare from worldly, perverted beauty and begin to recognize God's beauty again. "Finally, beloved, whatever is true, whatever is honorable, whatever is just, whatever is pure, whatever is pleasing, whatever is commendable, if there is any excellence and if there is anything worthy of praise, think about these things" (Philippians 4:8).

Like homing pigeons or lost dogs, we have an innate ability to identify and respond to God's beauty. "We have received . . . the Spirit that is from God, so that we may understand the gifts bestowed on us by God" (1 Corinthians 2:12). With the Spirit we can begin to recognize God's beauty all around us.

As Russell Willingham puts it, "We must learn to use our God-given powers of imagination to see the glory of Jesus Christ as revealed in Scripture. We need to envision his resplendent beauty. We need to see the compassion and mercy on his face. In doing this, we connect with the One our heart *actually* craves, rather than turning to a counterfeit with a pretty face and an hourglass figure."[*] This is our quest for the rest of this book.

---

[*]Russell Willingham, *Breaking Free* (Downers Grove, Ill.: InterVarsity Press, 1999), p. 61.

She moved with slumped posture from her sleeping compartment on the exterior wall into the inner room used for dining, cooking and entertaining. A narrow slit of moon and stars shone on the beaten clay through the rough wooden shutters. She moved with steps softer than the heavy breathing coming out of the room she passed on her left. She found no comfort on his pallet or her own this night. She left the relative warmth of her covers for the chill of the house—not so cold that her breath should come as clouds from her lips but enough so that presently a chill gripped her body, forcing her to clench her wrists and shiver. Just then a choppy snore interrupted the silence of this small residence located on the outskirts of an obscure Samaritan village.

Oh God. She still felt his breath biting at the skin on the back of her neck despite the distance between them. His presence lingered even after she retreated to the dining room and dipped some cool water from a clay jar, letting it roll down the hollow of her back to soak into the material of her nightgown. She did not know this man, really. The choice to be with him, in his house now, was made in haste. But since then haste had come to nest, for that was almost two years ago. At the time she felt this man, any man, was her only means to survival. It was not a good life. Now she wondered if it was really a life at all.

He was a scribe. He worked hard during the day. He was respected by some, tolerated by others. He was not loved. He made a living and was willing to share it with her in exchange for her body next to his. Every night he came home, ate dinner and led her to bed. This was her life.

Now, here in the hollow space of this inner room open only on one side through a narrow, shuttered window into a courtyard, she thought about crying. Water dripped from her fingers onto the dirt floor. She thought about going to the well during the heat of the next day to fetch water. She thought about neighbors snickering from inside windows and courts as she stole to the path at the edge of town. She thought about the day to come and decided she would not cry. There was no time to cry now, not in the dark. This was her time to be beautiful—invisible. In the darkness of this inner room she was not despised. She let herself live, breathe, some nights even worship. Yes, tonight she would worship.

She moved in silence, her feet ever hovering low across the dirt—a breath could not squeeze into the space. *Her feet and the dirt.* She stole a jar and wick from a shelf, ignoring the one placed in the window. In most houses the window would be lit; in this house it was intentionally forgotten. She moved in memorized patterns around furniture, her eyes open, blank, staring at nothing but grateful black. *Her feet and the dirt.* She placed the jar on the table. She gently lifted a scroll from another shelf, and she placed this too on the table.

Her feet and the dirt. This was her relationship with the earth—she walked on it and it left its dirt on her.

Now she sat. Nights like this one were the only times she really sat. During most days she moved. Dust would swirl around her feet and she would move before it settled. If she sat in the light the dirt would come to rest, and her thoughts would tear at her, and her heart would be torn. The daylight brought thoughts of failures and hurts, relationships broken by her and for her, ambitions that had shattered in her face.

She was cut by her ambitions at first, but soon their edges dulled. She looked for love, honor, children and reputation in a man—and she was cut. Then she looked for only love—another cut. Her body was torn, her dignity ripped; she looked for sympathy—the final cut. Her tears dried up. She looked for survival. That is what she did now; she survived, making decisions on immediate need and caring little for herself or others. During the days she looked for nothing. She survived in the dark.

She took a deep breath and lit the wick. A quick burst, then slowly growing into rhythmic flickering, the dim, orange flame lapped at the walls and washed the ceiling. This light was so different from the light of day—like being held by a father or cradled in a womb. It rose from the table like the cloaked arms of Moses at the Red Sea, and the darkness fled from its authority. This was her own private exodus from her world of slavery. She unrolled the scroll directly under her face, the lamp just to her left. In these pages of the law that the snoring man kept from his work she found her promised land. There was a God who promised sanctuary for everyone. She had even read a story about a prostitute serving him and being saved. This was her God. Maybe, just maybe, he loved her.

She worshiped him by moving her lips. No sound escaped her—barely a breath. These moments of contradiction with her God, as she secretly worshiped with dirty feet and shameful lips and all of her broken self in between, were the only moments she loved or felt loved. Time slipped by unnoticed.

She felt she might cry, this time for joy. She thought again of going to the well the next day under the bright noon sun. She huffed the lamp out, hovered silently to the shelf to return it, then to the table—*her feet and the dirt*—and returned the scroll to its shelf. She hesitated, looking through the open doorway into the man's sleeping apartment. He responded on cue with an abrupt snort. She turned and took her seat at the table and laid her head on her arms to sleep, her feet resting on the dirt.

*   *   *

The morning sun cracked through the shutters, and her beloved darkness fled to the corners of the room. She lifted her head from the table automatically as if a rooster had crowed inside her heart, "Wake up. Warm up. It is day, your day." As she rubbed the sleep from her eyes and felt the crease on her cheek, stirring came from the man's room. She forgot the voice from her heart that fled like a wisp of smoke in the wind. By the time the man entered the kitchen she was preparing breakfast as if she had been awake for an hour already.

"I woke up early this morning, refreshed. So I figured I would get an early start."

"Good. Good. I'm hungry this morning."

"Breakfast will be ready soon."

"There is much going on today with the council."

She nodded and kept about her preparations busily. He nodded. He respected her business. It was what drew him to her to begin with. He knew she would bring a cleanliness and order to his life that he had lacked since the death of his wife during the birth of their first child. The child had died with her. He found himself being grateful now, despite his extreme attempts not to be, that his son had not survived. He was further grateful that this woman was barren. She had been honest about that; barren, with many men to prove it. He was proud of his goodwill toward this woman—proud even that he allowed her the title "woman."

The man finished breakfast and left quickly with his materials for the day's work. She did not rest after he left. She stayed busy with household matters. She kept the most efficient home on that side of the village.

The sun was high now. The house warmed from the heat of the day. She looked at her water jar. She let go a sudden shiver despite the heat. No time for thought. No time for doubt.

The sun was hot indeed. She shaded her face by placing the large jar atop her head. Without looking to the left or the right she strode down the street trying to ignore whispers and snickering from neighbors' windows.

Finally she cleared the edge of the village, now a spectacle only for the sparse life of the wilderness. She bore the weight of the jar and the heat of the day with determined strength, and was grateful to be able to draw water without drawing condescending stares as well.

As she drew near the well of Jacob she saw a strange man, alone, with his back propped against a stone. This was an unwelcome situation. She wished he were not there, but at the same time she was curious. As she drew near the well she averted her eyes and began to pull the bucket to the surface. The stranger spoke.

"Give me a drink."

He spoke with the accent of a Jew. She glanced over at him. He was a Jew. His clothes made it obvious. She could not respond. This man was teasing her. *This man means me harm,* she thought. The Jews detested the Samaritans, and the Samaritans held no love for the Jews. She was afraid. Several men had hurt her before. She did not trust his request.

She glanced at the man again. Maybe he *was* thirsty. In her confusion she continued hoisting the bucket. Then she paused. This man had interrupted her silent loneliness. He was making requests of her. And he was a Jew. She was almost angry at this and yet still curious. With newfound courage she responded to the man.

"How is it that you, a Jew, ask a drink of me, a woman of Samaria?"

The man did not hesitate or even blink. "If you knew the gift of God, and who it is that is saying to you, 'Give me a drink,' you would have asked him, and he would have given you living water."

Now she knew that the man was having sport with her, so cross was his response. "Sir, you have no bucket, and the well is deep. Where do you get that living water? Are you greater than our ancestor Jacob, who gave us the well, and with his sons and his flocks drank from it?" She waited for a response. She knew that no Jew would claim to be greater than Jacob.

The man responded, "Everyone who drinks of this water will be thirsty again, but those who drink of the water that I will give them will never be thirsty. The water that I will give will become in them a spring of water gushing up to eternal life."

She hesitated again. The man did not sound condescending. He sounded like a friend or a father softly saying, "Peace, you are safe." She felt almost like she did in the hug of the candlelight less than twelve hours earlier. Maybe he was being truthful about this water. Maybe he was here to help. But she was still cautious. "Sir, give me this water, so that I may never be thirsty or have to keep coming here to draw water."

This time the man hesitated. He looked straight into her eyes. She was captivated, like a moth to a flame. Then he slowly nodded and spoke. "Go, call your husband, and come back."

This man tugged at her heart. She spoke suddenly as if being provoked or compelled under threat of life. "I have no husband." She startled herself with how loudly and desperately she spoke.

The man responded in his same comforting tone. "You are right in saying, 'I have no husband . . .' " She could see only her past. She was rocking herself in the corner of her father's house while blood pounded in the vessels of a blackened eye. The man still spoke. "For you have had five husbands . . ." She saw one husband after another in disgusting proximity. She had demanded too much or poured herself out hoping for change or expected too little or given herself too readily in hopes of love. The man still spoke. "And the one you have now is not your husband . . ." She saw herself sleeping at the kitchen table. Her eyes begged him to stop talking. He was digging up all that she had spent years burying. She was about to break. The man still spoke. "What you have said is true!" He was shaking her with his words. She wanted to plug her ears. She began to breathe so fast that her words piled into each other as she pushed them out. She had to fill this silence, stop her thoughts.

"Sir, I see that you are a prophet. Our ancestors worshiped on this mountain, but you say that the place where people must worship is in Jerusalem."

The man smiled and shook his head. He could not conceal his love for this Samaritan woman. It poured from his voice, his words, his face. He had seen down to the very soul of her. Somehow he knew her better than she had ever known herself, and he knew what to say. "Woman, believe me, the hour is coming when you will worship the Father neither on this mountain nor in Jerusalem. You worship what you do not know; we worship what we know, for salvation is from the Jews. But the hour is coming, and is now here, when the true worshipers will worship the Father in spirit and truth, for the Father seeks such as these to worship him. God is spirit, and those who worship him must worship in spirit and truth."

Her eyes lit up. She knew what it meant to worship in her spirit, deep down where no one else had been able to go until now. She knew of the hour to come. She understood what was being said, and like an excited little girl she burst. "I know that Messiah is coming. When he comes, he will proclaim all things to us."

The man standing beside her spoke. "I am he, the one who is speaking to you."

With those words, words so heavy and yet so light on her heart, she stumbled backward, kicking over her jar. Voices of other men approached from behind her. She did not take her eyes off of the face of the strange man who had asked her for a drink. Then she turned toward the village, grabbed up her long garment and began to run. She ran with gurgling eagerness, her soul crying, for she knew she was safe. She was home. Her dusty feet lifted high above the ground now and touched down upon the earth with graceful care. It was the same earth, it was the same pair of feet. But they had a different relationship now.[*]

---

[*]Adapted from John 4.

Chapter Four

Finding Respect

We have all been like the Samaritan woman of John 4. We beat ourselves down. We agree with other people's assessments of us. We use relationships to meet our needs. We discard people when they do not satisfy. We allow our failures and disappointments to define us. We allow others to abuse us, or we abuse them, in the hope of our own validation.

We need to experience the acceptance of Jesus in order to recognize God's beauty in us. To worship God in spirit and truth is to be beautiful, for we were made for it.

Jesus Offers Respect

The Samaritan woman could draw water with a bucket, but she had no effective tool for gathering respect. She had lost her name, her identity. She pieced together a form of respect by clinging to a man who could not satisfy, avoiding people, working nonstop, closing out the broken parts of herself and covering over her mistakes and hurts. Underneath it all she had lost respect for herself, and as an unavoidable result she lost respect for the people around her.

How can she, so convinced of the ugliness in and around her, recognize God's Spirit and truth in her? How can we? Alone she, and we, cannot without the intervention of a stranger at a well.

The Samaritan woman found respect for herself when Jesus gave her respect. Jesus spoke to her. He said things through his presence and expressions that we will never know. He respected her even when he knew everything about her.

Jesus' respect for the Samaritan woman immediately brings about drastic change. Before her encounter with Jesus she was despised by the people of the village. She drew water at midday to avoid the comments of her neighbors, who would normally draw water early in the morning. After her encounter with Jesus she darted into the town square, boasting with wild claims. "He couldn't be the Messiah, could he?" And people responded to her! Not only did she gain respect for herself, but the townspeople began to respect her as well. "Many Samaritans from that city believed in him [Jesus] because of the woman's testimony" (John 4:39).

What an amazing transformation in our woman at the well. Jesus gives her respect, she gives herself respect, and people recognize her transformation and give her respect as well. She has discovered God's beauty in herself—his Spirit and truth.

What About Today?

Respect is about receiving and then giving, not taking. Can we respect ourselves when our actions are guided by selfish desires? When we seize after respect as though it's our right to take it, we pervert respect in its pure form. Brennan Manning puts it this way: "Our huffing and puffing to impress God, our scrambling for brownie points, our thrashing about trying to fix ourselves while hiding our pettiness and wallowing in guilt are nauseating to God and are a flat denial of the gospel of grace."[*] If this is our path, then respect becomes less a gift and more a game; we have no choice but to use the tactics of competition, comparison, coercion and compromise.

Jesus' disciples had to be taught this lesson many times. Jesus caught

---

[*]Brennan Manning, *The Ragamuffin Gospel* (Sisters, Ore.: Multnomah Press, 2000), p. 20.

them arguing over who was the greatest among them; Jesus told them to be servants to each other and to extend respect even to small children. One disciple, John, surveyed his competition: "Teacher, we saw someone casting out demons in your name, and we tried to stop him, because he was not following us" (Mark 9:38). Jesus corrected the disciples again. Later the disciples prevented parents from bringing their children to Jesus to be blessed, and yet again Jesus confronted them.

Jesus is happy to give us respect if we will receive it. His disciples struggled with this concept just as we do, but Jesus was firm on the matter: "I am among you as one who serves" (Luke 22:27); "Love one another as I have loved you. No one has greater love than this, to lay down one's life for one's friends" (John 15:12-13).

The giving and receiving of respect gives birth to a wonderful phenomenon: friendship. Jesus speaks of this transformation in John 15:15: "I do not call you servants any longer, because the servant does not know what the master is doing; but I have called you friends, because I have made known to you everything that I have heard from my Father." Jesus does not remain merely "Rabbi" (a teacher) to his followers but becomes "Rabboni": a friend.

Enemies of Respect

Respect has to do with appreciation; God appreciates us as his creation and so gives us respect. We can compare two things and appreciate the differences and the similarities, and in so doing we can grow in our respect for both things. But when we compare things for any purpose other than appreciation, we remove respect from the equation. We reduce other people to milestones along the road to our self-realization: "I'm better than she is"; "I'll never be that attractive"; "Why does he get all the lucky breaks?" We split people into pieces that serve us and pieces that do not. Their mental prowess serves as a marker for us, while the rest of their being goes unnoticed. Their physical stamina or curvaceous figure overshadows their humanness. We objectify other humans to service our lustful desires or to rub salt on our own wounded self-image. In the process we kill off the respect we have for them and for ourselves.

Sometimes we have to discover through the callous teacher of experience that respect is not gained from a merely physical relationship. The physical body cannot create respect; the body receives respect or destroys it. Physical exchanges without accompanying spiritual and emotional exchanges result in ultimately hurtful and dehumanizing relationships.

Don't get me wrong; touch, as a physical expression of love, is important. But physical gestures should be expressions of respect that is already present, not attempts to gain or force respect. Until your physical gesture can exist purely as a gift and not a request, you are damaging respect, not gaining it. This is why God calls us to refrain from sex until we are married—in a covenant relationship that leaves little room for political gameplaying. Physical closeness tends to promise more intimacy than it can deliver on its own. In reality intimacy between people is achieved through closeness of two whole persons, and it takes time and care to develop the spiritual and emotional aspects of this closeness.

Compliments

We all want and need encouragement from others. This alone should be reason enough for us to strive to compliment others, but for some reason it isn't. So here is more: Giving compliments and encouragement to others helps us shift our focus from our perversion to God's beauty.

What is your first reaction to someone who exemplifies a character trait you wish you had? Inspiration? Motivation? Celebration? Often we react with resentment, jealousy, bitterness, sarcasm, hate, loathing, anger, lust or homicidal tendencies. (I exaggerate a little, but you get the point.) Complimenting others does not come naturally when our focus is on ourselves.

A Handbook for Complimenting Others

1. *Whom do you admire? Why? Let these people know why you admire them.*
2. *Keep a calendar to schedule acts of kindness or compliments for people in your life. Use a phone list or address book to begin. Mark birthdays and other important days for your friends in this calendar. Compliments take little time and energy:*
   - *Leave a funny message on someone's answering machine.*
   - *Drop off a word of encouragement at someone's door.*
   - *Mail someone a card.*
   - *Send someone an e-mail.*
   - *Wash the dishes or take out the trash for somebody else.*
   - *Write a letter to your parents.*
3. *Compliment people of both sexes, but be careful not to send unintended messages to people of the opposite sex. Flirting is different from complimenting. Ask friends of the same sex whether your compliments are crossing the line into flirtation.*
4. *As complimenting people you admire feels more natural to you, begin complimenting people outside your comfort zone.*
   - *Say something nice to the first person you see.*
   - *Talk with someone you don't normally talk with.*
   - *Thank someone working behind a desk or cash register.*

Other than singing loudly while driving, complimenting people is the best habit on earth. As you make complimenting and encouraging others a habit, your focus will shift away from yourself toward respecting others. And as you live in this new environment of respect, you will find yourself more and more aware of God's beauty in and around you.

Chapter Five
Body by Paul: Discipline & Boundaries

Often most young painters are taught what and how *not* to paint. They focus on their hand to keep it steady. They focus on the lines to stay within them. They focus on their successes and failures, learning pride or shame. All of this is self-centered. Everything about them as painters—all their successes and failures and accolades and harsh reviews—rides on their hand and only their hand.

This is not the way to paint beautifully, and it is not the way to live with purity. If we can learn that the nature of God's control and discipline is expansive and inspiring, not self-focused and negative, then the potential of our Christian lives is not suffocated and incomplete but rather guided by the infinite, creative beauty of God. Life, like painting, is an art informed as much by freedom and creativity as by discipline. While knowing the discipline of our hand and the boundaries of the lines we are to paint within, we must know also the vast and yearning spaces of the canvas and the guiding hand and freeing creativity of God.

Body by Paul

The apostle Paul helps explain the nature of God's boundaries and discipline.

> "All things are lawful for me," but not all things are beneficial. "All things are lawful for me," but I will not be dominated by anything.

"Food is meant for the stomach and the stomach for food," and God will destroy both one and the other. The body is meant not for fornication but for the Lord, and the Lord for the body. And God raised the Lord and will also raise us by his power. . . . Anyone united to the Lord becomes one spirit with him. Shun fornication! Every sin that a person commits is outside the body; but the fornicator sins against the body itself. Or do you not know that your body is a temple of the Holy Spirit within you, which you have from God, and that you are not your own? (1 Corinthians 6:12-14, 17-19)

I have a hard time reading 1 Corinthians. It contains a bunch of limits and guidelines—not popular items in today's society. Today's high values—freedom, equality, success, a full and satisfying life—are defined as "no limits." But as we come to learn, sometimes through pain and suffering, each of these values in reality is achieved and maintained through respecting boundaries and limits. How do we choose our limits? How do we maintain those limits? How do we start over after breaking them?

Nowhere does the Bible say, "Be disciplined and you will be saved." Paul does not offer boundaries to dictate our actions or cause us guilt and grief when we fail. Paul mentions boundaries as a means to change our focus from worldly beauty to God's beauty. "The body is meant not for fornication but for the Lord, and the Lord for the body." We need boundaries and discipline, but not for making us pure. We need them in order to keep our focus.

A Dictionary Definition of Fornication
Sexual intercourse between partners who are not married to each other.

This passage does not say "Don't sleep with a prostitute" as much as it says "You are members of Christ." This passage does not say "Don't fornicate" as much as it says "You are a temple." This passage is a list of blessings and promises, not a list of limits. We are members of Christ! I don't know exactly what that means, but I know that it is good. Christ accepts us, perversion and all, as a part of himself.

We are better off focusing on the character of God and what it means for us than focusing on our own unsure character that never measures up to our imagined expectations. Rather than investing all of our energies in restrictions and negative morality (what we shouldn't be), we should focus on the Lord and the things of the Lord.

We are temples of the Holy Spirit. We should not worry about stripping the temple walls bare as much as we should endeavor to cover them with pictures of God's beauty. What images help you to focus on God? It may be a gospel moment captured by a artistic genius like Rembrandt or van Gogh,

---

Check Your Temple Walls

1. *What slogans do you most often bear on your clothing?*
   a. *Brand names*
   b. *Things you find amusing*
   c. *Corporate logos*
   d. *Things or ideas you believe in*
2. *What decorations do you have hanging in your room?*
   a. *Objects or hobbies you enjoy*
   b. *Photographs or mementos of friends/family*
   c. *Celebrities or models*
   d. *Stuff you think is pretty*
3. *What motivates your clothing style and image?*
   a. *Fashion*
   b. *Statement*
   c. *Economy*
   d. *Belief*
4. *What are your top three activities for precious free time? Do people know you by these things? If not, how do people know you? Are you hiding your top three?*
5. *What thought are you most likely to return to in order to get you through the days, weeks and months of your life?*
   a. *A hobby you enjoy*
   b. *Your belief in Christ*
   c. *A person you love*
   d. *A fantasy you frequent*
6. *What changes to your temple walls (both spiritual and physical) do you need to make to be more conscious of God's beauty in and around you?*

---

or a picture scrawled by a niece or nephew. It may be a picture of friends or family or a special loved one. It may be a poster of Glacier National Park, a ski slope or a fly fisherman wading in a mountain stream.

What pieces or aspects of your life would you want displayed on the walls of God's temple? These things are God's beauty in you. The rest of the junk in our lives is perverted. You are a temple! Have you ever seen an ugly temple of God? I haven't.

What About When I'm Asleep? (Discipline, Schmiscipline!)

To every person who has tried to overcome something with all of his or her strength and has still failed, the word *discipline* might be rather stale to the ears. We have all experienced sin that seems to be involuntary—occurring completely against our choosing—so it is legitimate to ask, "How can I focus on God when I'm not even given the option or ability to choose?"

Allow me to paint the scene. The lights are dimmed. A muffled voice from across the room is repeating the phrase "Lord God" amid requests and praises. You sit with your head in your hands and your elbows resting on your knees. "Yes." You affirm the muffled prayer quietly and nod your head slightly. Gradually your thoughts begin to wander to your plans for the rest of the evening. All of a sudden your mind is accosted by a sweaty, X-rated cinematic second.

In my mind somewhere I have what I refer to as a "perverted picture file," made up of images blazed into my memory through TV, movies, magazines, conversations, repeated dreams and occasional experiences. I have spent many nights closing and then opening my eyes repeatedly, unable to sleep because of visions of violence, nudity and things without label pulled from my perverted picture file. They play inside my closed eyelids just as if I were turning on and off the TV. At least once I have feared falling asleep, not sure that I could endure hours of these episodes without waking up barking and frothing at the mouth, ready to be committed.

I say these things for the benefit of anyone else like me. We are freaks (and we are many), but God loves us. We can't be good apart from Jesus. In a way that's reassuring—we truly can't control our every thought—but it also proves the problem. Apart from Jesus we have each compiled our own perverted picture file.

We clearly need to curb the flow of these images (or unhealthy fantasies) into our mind. But the file is already plenty full, and we need to purge the images that are already there and those that enter unexpectedly. I made a breakthrough in this area when I realized that God never sleeps. To an all-powerful God what is the difference between when we are awake and when we are asleep? His beauty is still present, and our minds can still

We are freaks (and we are many), but God loves us.

access it. Likewise, he is still present, ready to respond to our prayers for more beautiful thoughts and visions. We still serve God as we sleep; we are merely serving him in a different manner.

With this in mind, try praying every night before you fall asleep, asking God to watch over you and protect you much like you would during the day. We did this when we were kids:

Now I lay me down to sleep,
I pray the Lord my soul to keep.

Pray that you will think beautiful thoughts that glorify him. In the morning thank him for another great night. If your file opened up on you again, ask him to forgive your sleeping sins and get them out of your head.

Sexual Sin: Curiosity, Selfish Fulfillment, Medication, Addiction

Sexual sin is an area of particular frustration for most of us. More rationalizing, groveling and yelling in our relationship with God occurs over these sins maybe than any others. Masturbation, pornography, premarital (or extramarital) sex, homosexual acts and sexual fantasies can be a grave we dig for our own spirits. For many of us these burials become a way of life. One thing is for sure—each of us struggles with sexual sin at a different level and in a different way. I have had conversations about these suffocating sins with several close friends. I have heard seasoned staff with InterVarsity share their struggles and failures. Male and female, young and old, single and married, we struggle with sexual sin.

I have struggled to different degrees and in different ways with masturbation, pornography, lust and fantasy. I have told myself that I was at a stage of development. I have masturbated just to get those desires out of me. I have looked forward to times of fantasy. I have hated myself for flipping through catalogs and magazines. I have forced myself to give money to the church every time I fell to sexual temptation. I have been excited to make it through one day without choosing sin. I have been shocked by stumbling after a year of "doing better." I have gone without showering to avoid masturbation. I have shared with friends in the hopes of being held accountable. I have cried, yelled, prayed, sworn, made vows and made threats. These things have not saved me from sin, but occasionally, in accordion fashion, these struggles have brought me closer to my Lord and Savior.

Even the apostle Paul cries out with us: "Wretched man that I am! Who will rescue me from this body of death?" (Romans 7:24). But in what seems to be a revolving door, Paul continues: "Thanks be to God through Jesus Christ our Lord!" (v. 25). Like Paul, I am forced to acknowledge that I am forgiven and loved even in the process of turning away from God. I cannot destroy God's love for me with my sexual sin.

For some the question may not be "Can God still love me when I sin?" but rather "Am I really doing anything wrong?" Sex is about discovery—uncovering our bodies and discovering beauty and intimacy. The hidden treasure in sex is another view of God's beauty in and around us. And we discover God through serving him. And we serve God through serving his creation. So sex is about serving others, and sex involves being served by others. We can know these things through God's Word, his creation and our own experience.

Male and female bodies illustrate that sex is about service. For pleasure to be maximum and mutual, each partner must serve the other. Each partner is vulnerable to and dependent on the other. When sex is turned into an act of personal gratification it is cheapened greatly. Since sex was created sacred—to be an act of service to help us know God better—then masturbation, fantasy, pornography and cavalier sexuality pervert God's beautiful creation and train us to pervert all of our relationships, including our relationship with God. Sexual sin is selfish self-medication, an addictive sin that leads eventually to betrayal.

How can I say this? When we sin sexually, we make a choice to satisfy our cravings over everything else. Whether we masturbate as a means of physical pleasure or as a form of emotional medication, we have put our-

---

Where Are You on the Scale of Sexual Addiction?

For most people sexual sin ranges from curiosity, to physical pleasure or selfish fulfillment, to medication, to sexual addiction.

1. What factors lead most often to your sinning sexually?
  a. Loneliness
  b. Physical drive (or hormones)
  c. Boredom
  d. Habit
2. How often do you struggle with sexual temptation?
  a. Only when I feel vulnerable
  b. When I'm stimulated by thought, sight, touch or some other stimulus
  c. Intermittently
  d. Regularly or almost constantly
3. What process do you go through while choosing to sin sexually?
  a. I agonize, sometimes crying
  b. I go through very little or no process
  c. I rationalize and speculate
  d. I arrange my lifestyle to facilitate it
4. How often or for how long are you able to avoid sexual sin once you have been tempted?
  a. I can wait, but I rarely abstain
  b. If I am going to do it, I do it right away
  c. I can put it off for weeks or months
  d. Often I don't try, if I do; I usually fail

selves in the position of the sole fulfiller and provider of our needs. This is an addictive self-image that isolates us relationally. In our addiction we betray ourselves (we were never meant to be our own provider), our God (his place as our provider has been taken away from him), and our potential future relationships (we will be less vulnerable and more self-oriented in relationships meant to be mutually giving).[*]

Accountability as a Means to Discipline

Perversion will suffocate us unless we have friends to get us out from under it. But many of us don't have friends we would trust with such intimate struggles. Our struggles with perversion are the last things we want to share with anyone.

---

[*]For more about the destructive nature of sexual addiction and steps you can take to defeat sexual sin, read Russell Willingham's *Breaking Free* (Downers Grove, Ill.: InterVarsity Press, 1999). His book has meant much to me.

There is great relief, however, in confessing our perversions to a close friend. What we think will make us feel dirty actually makes us feel cleaner. Confessing does much more than that though. Confessing our perversions provides more strength to resist them in the future. Our perversions beat us down and weaken us. We tell ourselves that we *are weak* and accept that we *will be* beaten by our perversions forever. Our friends know what weakness and defeat feel like, but they haven't been beaten by *our* perversions. Our friends have strength that they can give us just as we have strength that we can give them.

Confession of our perversions to a friend can also end loneliness. All too often we assume that no one around us would accept us if they knew what we really were. This is just not true. Other people are just as perverted as we are. This is why we need dear friends whom we know we can trust. When our perversions are out in the open they look smaller, less hairy, easier to squish. If we can step away from our perversions just far enough to realize that they do not define us, then we will realize that we will not cease to exist when they are torn away from us. Together with our friends, we can win.

For some, finding a safe friend may be even harder than confessing perversions. I am not suggesting we share something as controversial as a struggle with homosexuality or masturbation with everyone we know, or even every friend we have. We should be able to do this, but we can't. Our acquaintances, even our friends, may lack the awareness that they wrestle with perversions of God's pure beauty in their lives. Those still blind to their own perversions or not committed to our well-being may not respond with the love and understanding they should. These things take time and trust, as any intimate relationship would. Forming an intimate friendship may therefore require confessing less controversial sins first, before working up to the deeply wrenching stuff.

You are never alone in your perversion. By confessing we find that others thought they were alone as well. Even if our friends' struggles are not identical to ours, they are equal to ours.

But accountability is more than confession. Accountability gives us encouragement. To come to terms with our perversions we need to be reminded that they do not define us; just as light overcomes darkness, so God's beauty overcomes perversion. So we need friends who will love us and care for us when we cannot love and care for ourselves, who will remind us that God's beauty is brighter than our darkest deeds.

Baby Steps to Discipline

It is one thing to talk about discipline but another to be as disciplined as we would like. We need to take baby steps to discipline that will help us avoid situations where giving in to our perversions is inevitable. This requires us to recognize where our path to perversion begins. Does free time open a gate to your perversion? Do wandering thoughts and eyes lead you to sin? Does grumbling or arguing put you on the path to sin?

Try scheduling prayer times during times you are most likely to be tempted to sin sexually. Read a chapter of the Bible before you turn on the TV. Add symbols or reminders of your struggles with perversion to your personal time with God. I use a candle as a symbol of my covenant with God. Lighting it renews my covenant with him. As it burns I ask God to forgive my perversion and imagine it being burned up by the flame.

These are just a few examples. You will need to spend time with God and friends figuring out your own baby steps to discipline. But by definition baby steps are small and many. Discipline is not an easy or immediate thing. Do not turn against yourself when you continue to lack the discipline you desire, but keep taking those baby steps.

For those who have lived with sexual addiction for months or years, discipline takes on a greater urgency. Because sexual addiction is so encompassing—psychologically and physiologically—breaking those addictions will involve radical lifestyle changes. But the principle is still the same: perversion is a path that has led us away from God, and the best route back to God is traveled step by step.

Chapter Six

Offering Gratitude

Gratitude may be the most obvious and yet most neglected response to God's beauty. We become so entangled in our personal vendettas against perversion that we fail to notice the purity and beauty that God has given us. Worse yet, we notice God's investment in us and never think to give thanks.

Ingratitude Hurts You

Within the pages of the Old Testament the obscenity of ingratitude spills from the lips of the prophet Ezekiel.

> Thus says the Lord GOD to Jerusalem: Your origin and your birth were in the land of the Canaanites; your father was an Amorite, and your mother a Hittite. As for your birth, on the day you were born your navel cord was not cut, nor were you washed with water to cleanse you, nor rubbed with salt, nor wrapped in cloths. No eye pitied you, to do any of these things for you out of compassion for you; but you were thrown out in the open field, for you were abhorred on the day you were born.

Imagine being in the kind of need that Ezekiel describes in these verses: a baby thrown into an open field immediately after birth, crusted with sun-baked, rotten afterbirth, eaten slowly by ants, screaming and crying until your infant voice fades and your energy is gone. God speaks about us through Ezekiel's words to Jerusalem. In the face of eternity we are bloody, screaming babies wholly dependent on God's grace.

I passed by you, and saw you flailing about in your blood. As you lay in your blood, I said to you, "Live! and grow up like a plant of the field." You grew up and became tall and arrived at full womanhood; your breasts were formed, and your hair had grown; yet you were naked and bare.

I passed by you again and looked on you; you were at the age for love. I spread the edge of my cloak over you, and covered your nakedness: I pledged myself to you and entered into a covenant with you, says the Lord GOD, and you became mine. Then I bathed you with water and washed off the blood from you, and anointed you with oil. I clothed you with embroidered cloth and with sandals of fine leather; I bound you in fine linen and covered you with rich fabric. I adorned you with ornaments: I put bracelets on your arms, a chain on your neck, a ring on your nose, earrings in your ears, and a beautiful crown upon your head. You were adorned with gold and silver, while your clothing was of fine linen, rich fabric, and embroidered cloth. You had choice flour and honey and oil for food. You grew exceedingly beautiful, fit to be a queen. Your fame spread among the nations on account of your beauty, for it was perfect because of my splendor that I had bestowed on you, says the Lord GOD.

God loves us based on nothing that we have done. He loves us based on who he is. He has given you life in his image, his pledge, his covenant, his love, his dignity, his honor. He has cleansed, anointed and lavishly decorated you. He has called you exceedingly beautiful, fit to be a queen (sorry guys). He has given you his glory to do with as you will.

But you trusted in your beauty, and played the whore because of your fame, and lavished your whorings on any passer-by. (Ezekiel 16:3-15)

God has acted beautifully toward us, and any response that neglects gratitude toward him, the source of all our good gifts, is a betrayal of his kindness to us. When we give ourselves credit for the good in our lives or attribute that good to everyone but God, when we focus on our failing struggle for pure hearts and beat ourselves to a pulp over our impure bodies, we misrepresent reality and mistreat God.

Where has God brought you from? What has he given you that you did not even know to ask for? With what people has he blessed you? What beauty looks ugly to you because of your ingratitude? Recognizing God's beauty takes only the simple act of gratitude, a willingness to thank God for being God.

Ingratitude Hurts Others

Has God ever failed anyone? Has he ignored cries or denied requests for days, months, years? Does it seem as though God withholds himself from some people while revealing himself to others? Do you doubt that God is good when you see people struggle or suffer?

These are painful questions, and the answers sometimes even more so. I have dear friends and family who have hurt for years from these questions and their answers. It does not seem fair; God appears to be indifferent and even unjust in his casual favoritism.

It is so easy—so human—to be dissatisfied when life is anything less than exactly what we want. I know this well; I expect complete health at all times. If I catch a cold I become agitated, angry, discontent and eventually discouraged. I expect time and circumstance to bend to my every whim. When they do not, I am completely nonplussed. I am quickly irritated by projects that don't go well; I am easily hurt by unkind words and deeds.

Then I run into someone who is enduring extreme pain from chemotherapy, or someone whose memory has been lost to injury or disease. And I realize that I am a baby flopping about in my own pathetic mucus—dependent on God for a safe home, decent clothes, life—all of which he has given me gladly.

What does God really owe us, anyway? It is God, after all, not some deal-maker selling favors to the highest bidder. The writer of Ecclesiastes 7:13-14 understood this:

Consider the work of God;
    who can make straight what he has made crooked?
In the day of prosperity be joyful, and in the day of adversity consider;
God has made the one as well as the other, so that mortals may not
find out anything that will come after them.

God gives us much beauty, but he does not owe us anything. People may blame themselves for their sins and their harmful effects; they may blame God for being absent or distant. Most likely they blame both. But no matter how tragic life gets, we have God to thank for giving us life and an image of his beauty.

From this section's title you may be expecting a discussion of how our ingratitude hurts the people around us. Well, in a way I have done so. Discouragement prospers where gratitude is void. Even though discouragement most dramatically affects the person directly experiencing it, it causes collateral damage to the loved ones of the afflicted. Discouragement—a void of gratitude—reverts our focus off of God's beauty and back onto our perverted selves. We don't respond to the needs of others when we are obsessed with our needs and the unfairness of our situation. We don't care as much about the hurt others feel when we are hurt, even though their hurt often comes through our own. God's beauty becomes harder for our friends to see when we cloud the air around us with our ingratitude.

Ingratitude Hurts God

Natalie daydreamed of hugging her father at lunchtime. He was coming to have lunch with her in the lunchroom, with all the other children watching. She would be the only one eating with her father. She wrote of her parents hugging her between them on a picnic in Chicago with her cat, Emily. She drew a picture for her father.

Natalie was a special artist. She was patient for a first grader. She enjoyed details, even if they were indecipherable to everyone else. That morning she drew a picture of her father in his brown recliner. Emily was curled up on a heap of laundry in the middle of the floor. Natalie's father was big, almost too big for the chair.

"Where are you in the picture, Natalie?" I asked her.

"Oh, I am in the corner. Being very quiet."

"In the corner?" My heart began to beat slightly faster.

"My father has headaches. I must be very quiet when my father has headaches."

I frowned. "Oh, your father gets bad headaches?"

"He drinks medicine from a bottle and sits very still before work, before I walk to school. Sometimes my mother packs my lunch. I pretend to be an invisible fairy and sneak outside."

"Wow, I bet that would make an interesting picture too." I took a last look at the picture of her father in his chair. He was holding his "medicine" in his right hand. There were more medicine bottles on the floor. I didn't want to go any further in the conversation.

Natalie was dressed in one of her father's dress shirts. It was wrinkled and hung untucked down to her knees. She had missed one of the buttons toward the bottom so that the buttonhole side hung down three inches further than the other side, which buckled slightly. She had folded the collar down well in the front, but the back was standing up.

Her hair was uncombed as always. She had pretty, long blonde hair. It dangled endlessly in her way. She blew at it with her lips. She pulled at it with her hands. She did not dislike her hair. It was almost a joke she told over and over. She would smile and sigh, "My hair will just never behave."

She started to make a bead bracelet for her father, but as lunch drew near she became "elbow happy." Her limbs began to flail about with increased energy. She eventually surrendered all hopes of finishing her bead bracelet and began to jump and chant.

"My father is coming. My father is coming to lunch. Lunch, lunch, lunch, lunch, lunch with me."

"Ssshhh. Natalie, you need to settle down." It was a reactionary response. I didn't really mean it; she was a pure joy to watch bounding about. Then I chilled. Her father *must* come to lunch. I could not let my mind picture what would happen if he did not. I prepared for lunch. *Lunch, lunch, lunch, lunch, lunch with me,* I thought.

Students finished their lunches and dumped the picked-over remains in the garbage as they peeled out toward the playground. Natalie sat quietly, alone. She had no lunch. Her father was supposed to bring it. Lunch was almost over. No one came for her. She did not complain, or cry, or even frown. I imagined her sitting quietly in her corner while even her cat could curl close to her father's chair. I left the lunchroom in tears.

Natalie's unwillingness to love her father any less created overwhelming and repeated heartbreak in her life. Have you ever thought of God as being like little Natalie? God's unconditional love for us makes him very vulnerable. When we bellow and moan, lash out at God, tell him to be quiet and stay in his corner while we drink of our bitterness, he will do what we say. He will not overpower or cause us to do something by force.

When we forget God and go about our business, God patiently sits waiting for us to return his love, which remains unabated. God takes the first step in relating to us. He has risked first. He brought us into being and watched us turn away from him and look elsewhere for life and beauty. He sent his Son to give us respect, saying, "Perhaps they will respect him" (Luke 20:13). Like a dear friend leaving without a farewell gift, we leave God more alone than before he created us. "And the LORD was sorry that he had made humankind on the earth, and it grieved him to his heart" (Genesis 6:6). Yet God still loves us and waits for us. That is what makes him purely beautiful, worthy of our gratitude.

Record Your Gratitude

1. How did you realize you needed God? What changes did God begin making in you? How have you seen him intervene in your life? How have you strayed from him? How has he shown his continued acceptance of you? Write down the details of your life with God. If you cannot answer these questions, ask a friend to help.

2. List the people who have loved you and helped you grow. How did they come into your life? Did you seek them out? Did you choose them? Did they choose you? Did God have a hand in their being there for you?

3. "I planned on . . . but God's plans were . . ." Fill in this formula as many times as you can.

4. Remember the three worst times in your life. List benefits and positive effects that came out of these times.

5. Thank God for every thing you have written so far. Thank other people where possible.

6. Record every case in which God has broken a promise to you. If you come up with any, first ask God to defend himself, then ask a friend to help you through prayer and Scripture to relate God's defense to you.

Chapter Seven

The Necessary Life of Passion

High school. In my senior year I met the girl I eventually planned to marry. She was visiting relatives who attended my church—staying for three months. She was smart, attractive, outgoing, Christian. She was looking for friends. I showed her around town. Soon we were spending hours at the botanical gardens, in my car on country back roads and wherever we could be alone together.

She colored my life with bright paint. We were teens tired of dull colors; it had to be bright or nothing. Our beliefs and upbringing gave us lines to paint in, but our brush strokes were increasingly feverish, uncontrolled, untrained. We breathed each other's breath for hours at a time, revealing to each other more and more of God's canvas that was our flesh, body and soul.

By God's mercy we were spared from the full potential of unleashed passions and hormones. After three months she returned home, thousands of miles away. The distance brought sobriety and eventually guilt. We determined to correct our course.

We decided to use darker outlines and smaller brushes, smaller strokes. Maybe black and white was better than color anyway. We created a treatise and signed it: pages of legal talk and specific directions for every scenario: It went on something like this.

OK in Public:	OK in Private:	Miscellaneous:
• *hand to face*	• *hand to head*	• *lips to lips are never permitted*
• *hand to hand*	• *lips to hand*	• *hugs can be full but brief*
• *lips to cheek or forehead*		• *bodies must remain still*

In some circumstances the treatise worked, but like the Pharisees of the New Testament we often found ways to interpret it differently or dismiss it. After two years of this careful and stilted relational painting, we realized that the work of art made between us was anything but graceful. We had problems. I wasn't sure how to love with bright, strong colors anymore. Finally we put the painting of our relationship aside; work on it was finished. It was what it was, and It would never be anything more.

Lines and Spaces

In some ways I am still trying to regain my feeling for painting—loving and living. I sometimes can't allow myself enough freedom to make bold and daring strokes of the brush. What if I make a mistake? What if I go outside the lines? But the only way to paint beautifully, to have beautiful relationships, is to know the lines well but the spaces better—to know the limitations of your hand and brush but also the infinite capabilities of God's creative Spirit in you.

The only way to paint beautifully, to have beautiful relationships, is to know the lines well but the spaces better.

In a sense, God has already made each painting; after all, we cannot create anything apart from him. We are the lines, the limitations. He has given us the spaces, the possibilities. He has made us painters. Our fullest potential for creating beautiful life is to learn his style, his technique, his use of color, shadow, shading, brushstroke and contrast.

Passion Over All

Passion is necessary for loving other people, but by its nature passion is scary, always straining toward the outer limits. God is the creator of passion; it comes to us when we encounter God himself—personal, present and unrelenting in his love for us. Without this passion, we at best hobble down the relentless road of obedience. Josiah (the boy king of the Old Testament) was able in a limited and stilted manner to do what was right out of an obscure conviction, a sense of loyalty to his heritage and a keen awareness of the lessons of history. It was not until he met God personally that he realized the true extent of his sin and its effect, and the urgency of cleaning it up. We are not left the option of knowing God and remaining passionless.

Passion is the locomotive for the necessary response to the greatest of commandments: "Love the LORD your God with all your heart, and with all your soul, and with all your might" (Deuteronomy 6:5). We cannot live a life of beauty or purity without passion. Josiah encountered God through hearing the words of a forgotten book of the law. David often encountered God through psalms of praise, pleading or protest. Jacob encountered God through a vision and then later through a physical encounter.

Whatever the means, encountering God charges all of our actions and motivations with passion. We will make mistakes, but if we live in the passion of our encounter with God, we will be able to say with our ancestors in the faith, "In my life I have done much good and much foolishness, but from that day to this I have done it all for the Lord."

An Aside
A Lesson in Passion

Shaphan would tell me stories of the boy king Joash, who began his reign at the age of seven. Only a child myself, I often wondered what it would have been like to be raised in secret like Joash—just a temple boy, not a prince.

I was eight when I became king. My father was killed at the age of twenty-four by his own servants. Those servants were in turn killed by the people of Judah. This was what I was thrust into, what I came to rule as a boy. Unlike Joash, I did not have a temple upbringing or a priest to instruct me. I had only a handful of servants who had not betrayed my father. Of these, most knew only the evil oppression of my grandfather Manasseh.

Only my secretary Shaphan seemed to stem from times earlier than his own years. With everyone else barred from the room, I would devour his "lessons" for hours on end. He told me of the great kings David and Solomon, who ruled the undivided kingdom. He taught me much about the worthy rule of my great-grandfather Hezekiah, and how all of his reforms were lost under the dark times of his son Manasseh. Shaphan even taught me about Ahab of Samaria, and how now the North had been lost—Samaria, the cost of disobedience. And so as a child I decided to reign like the great kings. I decided to follow the God of my ancestors who so long ago had brought us from Egypt and given us this land, who had given me this land to rule.

In all things I labored to observe the commandments passed down to us from Moses. I followed what I knew with respect and discipline. But I lacked conviction. I could not see the evidence of my own sin or the sin of my people. I did not understand how, like putrid smoke, sin burned the eyes of our God. I did not know him as a person. I could not see his tears or his anger. I knew him only as an ancient king whose wishes were to be honored if it were to go well with the land. Lord, forgive me, I did not know you in my heart.

But there was a man in Jerusalem, Hilkiah the high priest, who had been commissioned by godly men before him to preserve the book of the law until the shadow of Manasseh had withdrawn from the land, for my grandfather had persecuted the followers of the Lord. I had reigned for eighteen years when Hilkiah perceived that I was a king after the great kings and not under the shadow of Manasseh. He chose to reveal the words of the law.

I had sent Shaphan to Hilkiah to make provisions for the repair of the temple, just as the boy-king Joash had. When Shaphan returned to me, he shook like an olive tree with an ax put to its base. Sweat dripped like dew from his nose and chin with each shudder. He began his report in a droning voice: "Your servants have emptied out the money that was found in the house, and have delivered it into the hands of the workers who have over-sight of the house of the Lord." Then he paused, leaning slightly forward to indicate that he had more to say.

With a nod I bid him continue, and I noticed that with a great effort, as though bearing a tremendous weight, he clutched a scroll to his left side under his robe. I frowned. What was all this sheepishness in a man whose candor I so often depended on? All at once he spoke again, lifting and unrolling the scroll. "The priest Hilkiah has given me a book." Then, shakily at first, he began to read to me the words that had brittled his bones.

I do not remember breathing or looking away from Shaphan as he read. The words pouring from the mouth of God through this man—my secretary Shaphan, who had told me so many stories before—pierced my heart and soul.

Hear, O Israel: The LORD is our God, the LORD alone. You shall love the LORD your God with all your heart, and with all you soul, and with all your might. Keep these words that I am commanding you today in your heart. Recite them to your children and talk about them when you are at home and when you are away, when you lie down and when you rise. Bind them as a sign on your hand, fix them as an emblem on your forehead, and write them on the doorposts of your house and on your gates.

When the LORD your God has brought you into the land that he swore to your ancestors, to Abraham, to Isaac, and to Jacob, to give you—a land with fine, large cities that you did not build, houses filled with all sorts of goods that you did not fill, hewn cisterns that you did not hew, vineyards and olive groves that you did not plant—and when you have eaten your fill, take care that you do not forget the LORD, who brought you out of the land of Egypt, out of the house of slavery. The LORD your God you shall fear; him you shall serve, and by his name alone you shall swear. Do not follow other gods, any of the gods of the peoples who are all around you, because the LORD your God, who is present with you, is a jealous God. The anger of the LORD your God would be kindled against you and he would destroy you from the face of the earth. (Deuteronomy 6:4-15)

As Shaphan finished reading, releasing me from my trance, I fell lamely to my knees. My heart and my throat were torn open, but all that escaped me was a halting whimper. A man of only twenty-six years, a king for eighteen, I fell before my God with a throaty squeak and a whimper.

I clenched the hair of my scalp in my fingers to lift my head toward heaven as though beckoned. *Oh Lord, I have not known you in my heart; now you burn every inch of it with fire. I have not loved you with all my soul; now my soul is crushed by your terrible love.* My might was taken from me. My chin quaked. My lips shuddered. Through clenched eyes, tears sped down my cheeks and neck toward the collar of my garment. With a burst of anger and zeal I tore the garment down the middle, leaving it dangling off my shoulders and around my waist. With *this* might, the might of the Lord *my* God, I would love him. With all that he had given me, I would love him.

These words of the law still grasped me like huge hands—strong, dangerous hands, but with only good intent. Intent to shape and mold. These words were the anvil and hammer. God's breathing of them was the bellows. I felt his breath on me. Why had my father not shared these words with me? Why had I not seen them bound or inscribed anywhere in the land of Israel? How had we been allowed to forget them so quickly?

"Because the LORD your God, who is present with you, is a jealous God." The words would not release me, and to this day still have not. That day I discovered the passion of a God who was personal, a God who was present, a God who would never release me to any other. In that passion I do all things with joy for the service of my God. In my life I have done much good and much foolishness, but from that day to this I have done it all for the Lord.[*]

*   *   *

Prayer Fuels Passion

A major instrument of passion in our lives is prayer. The psalmist cries out to God as Creator, Redeemer, Savior, Lord and Judge. Job bellows at God for justification. Many times the need for prayer comes when we are at our rawest, in the midst of failure, shame, disgust and brokenness. We need to banish the thought that there are times when God doesn't want to hear from us. Never are we too dirty to lift ourselves up to God in prayer; he gladly dusts off our bloody knees with his bloody hands, and we are healed.

Being able to pray in the middle of a sinful activity has been a powerful help for me. Even when I want to sin, I find hope and healing when I pray, "Jesus, help me. Help me not to want this anymore." Russell Willingham

---

[*]Adapted from 2 Kings 22.

gives a beautiful model prayer for potentially sinful situations.

> Lord, I see that woman in the short skirt, and it feels as if her embrace would love all my pain away. It's a deception. She cannot meet my need for love. My own wife, as affectionate as she is, cannot fill it. Lord, I need YOU. You are the lover of my soul and the only one who can quench this insatiable thirst of mine.
>
> I don't need a woman to wrap herself around me in order to feel loved and significant—I need your arms. And I thank you, Lord Jesus, that when I come running to you in my broken, sinful state you wrap those arms around me, just like the father of the prodigal son.[*]

Inevitably we will pray to God to purify us and then find ourselves still perverted. We will pray and fail to the point of callousness. Often this has led me to anger. I become incensed at God, ranting and raving and crying and moaning and shaking my fist, wondering if he doesn't care or cannot help. This is still prayer. Our complaints are at least keeping the conversation going with God. When he wants to get a word in, he will. If you were God, would you rather have people rail honestly in your face, or would you rather they fume in quiet and then blow some religious gas at you every now and then? Our goal in striving to be pure is not to be good or to please God but to recognize him and know him. Our failures may not make us "good," but they can help us become pure by helping us turn toward God.

Our failures may not make us "good," but they can help us become pure by helping us turn toward God.

A Word of Summary: Finding Balance in Beauty
The book of Ecclesiastes looks with us for a middle road between closing our eyes to all of God's beauty and opening our eyes to all of our perverted

---

[*]Russell Willingham, *Breaking Free* (Downers Grove, Ill.: InterVarsity Press, 1999), pp. 172-73.

corruptions of that beauty, a middle road lit by passion and pointed toward pure beauty:

> In my vain life I have seen everything; there are righteous people who perish in their righteousness, and there are wicked people who prolong their life in their evildoing. Do not be too righteous, and do not act too wise; why should you destroy yourself? Do not be too wicked, and do not be a fool; why should you die before your time? It is good that you should take hold of the one, without letting go of the other; for the one who fears God shall succeed with both. (Ecclesiastes 7:15-18)

Travelers on the middle road strive for God's perfect beauty and accept his grace for their perversions. Why starve yourself of beauty and wonder when joy and pleasure are part of God's perfect plan? Why bludgeon your senses with every promise, however dubious, of pleasure and desire you encounter? The Bible offers the possibility of balancing between the two, a good life of taking hold of God's beauty and wonder without letting go of discipline and self-control.

Chapter Eight

Relating to the Other Sex

We are a generation of swingers. People in every coffee shop, nightclub and grocery store are swinging or wanting to swing right now.

What do I mean by swing? I mean living life at full swing.

Jesus came to give us free and full lives (John 8:36; 10:10; 15:11). Theologically this has to do with the truth behind our existence and our purpose. But what does it look like Friday night? People who know love, sacrifice, selflessness and surrender ought to be having an awesome time. People who know Jesus have faith and trust and forgiveness and grace and mercy and hope and peace.

> Christians ought to be celebrating constantly. We ought to be preoccupied with parties, banquets, feasts, and merriment. We ought to give ourselves over to veritable orgies of joy because we have been liberated from the fear of life and the fear of death. We ought to attract people to the church quite literally by the fun there is in being a Christian.[*]

Of all the people on this earth, Christians should swing the most freely.

---

[*]Robert Hotchkins, quoted in Brennan Manning, *The Ragamuffin Gospel* (Sisters, Ore.: Multnomah Press, 2000), p. 143.

Why Do I Crave Other Humans?

Our need to connect with others at a spirit-to-spirit level is what drives us to swing. But as much as swinging is symptomatic of a desire to relate to others, I daresay that we pursue relationships because we desire to make contact with our Creator God.

Think about the last romantic movie you saw. Every moment in that movie leads up to a point when the two stars finally find eternity in each other. "Eternity," as filmmakers would have you believe, is a moment so consuming that you can finally forget about the past and the future. Nothing in life matters anymore beyond this other person. A lifelong search for a moment of peace is available only through this other person. And *now* these two are eternally together. We don't find out whether a few months from *now* they marry or break up, because a few months from *now* doesn't matter. The movie *Never Been Kissed* describes such a moment of eternity:

> That thing, that moment, when you kiss someone and everything around you becomes hazy and the only thing in focus is you and this person and you realize that that person is the only person that you are supposed to kiss for the rest of your life. And for one moment you get this amazing gift and you want to laugh and you want to cry, 'cause you feel so lucky that you found it and so scared that it will go away all at the same time.

So is all of eternity really wrapped up in one moment with another person? Where does God fit in all of this?

People carry with them the image of God. And in our hunt for the everlasting moment of perfect peace and belonging we are frisking others for a taste of God. But we get only a wisp, a shadow. We are too afraid or unwilling to ask God for peace, love and mercy, so we try to take them from others. We practically squash people onto a spiritual juice grind to suck out every bit of God we can get. Then we move on, leaving behind us the pulp of our pillage.

We swing to find a lost God, a God we seek and run from at the same time. The taste of eternity here on earth we so often seek can only truly be found when we recognize our desire is for the Creator *in* the creation.

Having found this God, having realized this desire, Christians should be swinging harder and longer than anyone.

Why Do I Crave the Other Sex?

God is relational—three persons in one: Father, Son and Spirit. Human relationships, intersecting images of God, help us to experience and understand our relational God. But why do we seek these relational experiences with the other sex? It seems that men possess something women need, and women possess something men need.

> So God created humankind in his image,
>   in the image of God he created them;
>   male and female he created them. (Genesis 1:27)

This verse gives us a clue as to our sexual nature. The repetition here is not just poetry. Not only are individual males and females made in the image of God; the distinctive and specific characteristics of "maleness" and "femaleness" were created in the image of God as well. This does not mean that God is sexual; he is not female or male or androgynous. It means that human beings of both sexes, distinct as they are, carry God's image.

Maleness and femaleness are bound together in Genesis 2:24: "Therefore a man leaves his father and his mother and clings to his wife, and they become one flesh." Not only maleness and femaleness but the relationship between them reflect God's image. God designed and created this arrangement.

So we desire to relate to the other sex because in doing so we can know God better. Of course, this root desire can be buried deep below the fact that we think the other sex is sexy, funny, cute, wonderful, attractive . . .

How Can I Think at a Time Like This?

Before we can swing freely in pure and fulfilling relationships, we need to be in touch with God. We need to follow the basic guidelines he has set for us in his Word. We need to know how he is shaping us to relate. We need to know our limitations, including the weaknesses in our relationship with him. We need to know how our relating to the other sex will flourish given our culture, our conscience and our personalities.

Once we are in relationships we need to continually ask ourselves if we are being honest about the balance between our passion and our commitment. If we blindly enter relationships with the other sex, we surrender our ability to differentiate between God's beauty and our perversions. Many people are careful not to wound or be wounded in relationships, but how many people are careful not to ignore or neglect? But if we avoid the other sex altogether we surrender our full potential to know God and recognize his beauty through others and through relationships. So swing with the other sex, but swing with care.

Chapter Nine

I Want to Swing, but I'm Not Sure How to Dance

Dating . . . courtship . . . I am not interested in grandstanding on the side of any one form of relating between the sexes. I have tried just about all of them. All of them worked, and none of them worked. I have related well, and I have related poorly. I have healed, and I have hurt. It doesn't seem to matter what form of relating I use. It depends more on

- my relationship with Scripture
- my relationship with God
- my relationship with myself
- my relationship with the Holy Spirit
- my relationship with my culture

These relationships shape our choices as we relate to the other sex.

What Does the Bible Say?

The Bible does not tell us to kiss only on the fourth date or to begin a courting relationship only once we are 86.3% sure that we want to get married or to relate to the other sex only in groups or to do certain things only during the day. But the Bible definitely has some relevant things to say.

Sex belongs in marriage. "Save yourselves!" The unremitting cry from youth pastors and parents to wait until you're married still echoes in many minds. Others regret that no one cared enough to tell them to wait. Probably we all wish that someone had *shown* us, explained *why* waiting is so important.

God created the sexes. Human Eve was sexually different from human Adam, and these different sexes were created exclusively for each other, to form the first human relationship. This basic human relationship, an informal marriage, is given further definition: "Therefore a man leaves his father and his mother and clings to his wife, and they become one flesh" (Genesis 2:24). The marriage relationship replaces (to an extent) paternal and maternal relationships. And with the phrase "become one flesh" God links the physical event of sex to the relationship of marriage. Our parents and youth pastors saw all that rides on this one relationship: joining physically and sexually is meant to be an indicator—a signature—that the relationship is finally and totally sealed as a common life. The term "premarital sex" would not have made sense because to have sex with a person was to be married to that person. The Bible instead speaks of adultery: sexual relations that divide one flesh in several directions.

Fantasies and the thought life. The impact of fantasies comes through in Proverbs 6:27-28:

Can fire be carried in the bosom
  without burning one's clothes?
Or can one walk on hot coals
  without scorching the feet?

When it comes to our thoughts, Scripture is unbending. "You have heard that it was said, 'You shall not commit adultery.' But I say to you that everyone who looks at a woman with lust has already committed adultery with her in his heart" (Matthew 5:27-28). Our minds are to be fixed on God's pure beauty, not traveling down any perverted path that entices us with false beauty. This holds true for men finding themselves attracted to women for the wrong reason as well as women forming unrealistic or unhealthy expectations of men.

Lack of self-control carries a price. Lacking self-control leaves us and the people around us exposed and vulnerable to hurt. But self-control is not so much a matter of isolating yourself from some people and surrounding yourself with others. Self-control has to do with controlling yourself: being careful about *how* you relate to others. Paul seems to tell us to avoid people who don't believe what we believe:

> Do not be mismatched with unbelievers. For what partnership is there between righteousness and lawlessness? Or what fellowship is there between light and darkness? (2 Corinthians 6:14)

but not before he tells us who *not* to avoid.

> I wrote to you in my letter not to associate with sexually immoral persons—not at all meaning the immoral of this world . . . since you would then need to go out of the world. (1 Corinthians 5:9-10)

Instead he tells us to guard ourselves against those who claim to believe what we believe but whose lives suggest different ideas:

> Now I am writing to you not to associate with anyone who bears the name of brother or sister who is sexually immoral or greedy, or is an idolator, reviler, drunkard, or robber. Do not even eat with such a one. (1 Corinthians 5:11)

An unbalanced intimate relationship spells disaster for both parties. We invite disaster by seeking high intimacy with an unbeliever, for true intimacy shares a balance of our spiritual, mental, emotional and physical being with another. How can intimacy be achieved with someone who does not believe in, understand or know our God? The only common element of intimacy left to share is the physical, and without the other elements this is disaster. Likewise, we invite disaster by seeking high intimacy with people who pay lip service to God but do not seek after his pure beauty.

Self-control applies most intimately to our private lives. Do your private actions, which seem honest enough in the dark, become grotesque when exposed to the light? Our secret perversions cannot survive the brightness of God's pure beauty.

How far is too far? Disrespect and disgrace, violation and abuse, dishonor and exploitation—going too far leads to these things. If you can behave in a manner that does not disrespect, disgrace, dishonor or exploit God, your friend or yourself, then your behavior is within biblical bounds (1 Thessalonians 4:3-7). Paul offers a value to replace these vices. "But fornication and impurity of any kind, or greed, must not even be mentioned among you, as is proper among saints. Entirely out of place is obscene, silly, and vulgar talk; but instead, let there be thanksgiving" (Ephesians 5:3-4).

Deciding whether behavior is disrespectful, disgraceful, dishonorable or exploitive is a complex process involving your relationships with God, yourself, the Holy Spirit and your culture. The apostle Peter warns us as much: "Beloved, I urge you as aliens and exiles to abstain from the desires of the flesh that wage war against the soul" (1 Peter 2:11). We relate to others in the midst of a war between God's beauty and our perversion. Even as we long to give to others as God has given to us, we struggle with a desire to take for ourselves whatever we can get.

Take Heart and Then Give Heart

Our relationship with God is reflected in our obedience to him and our treatment of other people. The apostle John spells it out for us: "Now by this we may be sure that we know him, if we obey his commandments" (1 John 2:3). He follows this up by saying, "This is his commandment, that we should believe in the name of his Son Jesus Christ and love one another" (1 John 3:23). So a look at our relationship with God begins with a look at our love for others.

The Bible is full of passages that tell us how to love one another. We benefit greatly in our choices regarding how to relate by studying these passages. We learn from Romans 14:13, 19 that others have failings much like our own; rather than condemning them we can assist. "Let us therefore no longer pass judgment on one another, but resolve instead never to put a stumbling block or hindrance in the way of another. . . . Let us then pursue what makes for peace and for mutual upbuilding."

God himself provides the model for relating to others in Philippians 2:3-5: "Do nothing from selfish ambition or conceit, but in humility regard others as better than yourselves. Let each of you look not to your own interests, but to the interests of others. Let the same mind be in you that was in Christ Jesus."

Wow. This is the furthest thing from normal for us. Only intimacy with God and a close daily walk with his Son can bring about this loving attitude toward others: "Love is patient; love is kind; love is not envious or boastful or arrogant or rude. It does no insist on its own way; it is not irritable or resentful; it does not rejoice in wrongdoing, but rejoices in the truth. It bears all things, believes all things, hopes all things, endures all things" (1 Corinthians 13:4-7). Peter sums it all up: "For the Lord's sake . . . honor everyone. Love the family of believers. Fear God" (1 Peter 2:13, 17).

We must never forget that our ability to love others genuinely and deeply depends on our relationship with God: "Now that you have purified your soul by your obedience to the truth so that you have genuine mutual love, love one another deeply from the heart" (1 Peter 1:22). We must be active in our relationship with God before we can have purely loving relationships with others.

Who Am I? Who Is God Shaping Me to Be?

Each of us relates differently in different situations. Some of us long for stress and excitement; others long for peace and calm. Some of us hunger for smaller groups or one-on-one conversation, while others crave big crowds. How you enjoy relating to people suggests how you will relate most comfortably and therefore most authentically.

Do you enjoy lots of people lots of the time? Would you rather talk than party? Do you need time to yourself to do your own thing? Would you rather be with one friend all the time? Are you able to share more when a mutual commitment is in place? Do you get caught up in excitement so much that you forget about those around you? Do you like to hang out and then decide what to do? Do you like to make plans before getting together? Do you like to measure your commitments before getting involved in new relationships? Do you prefer to follow your heart when relating with people? Do you live in the present? Do you worry about the long-term effects of your actions? Do you second-guess yourself? Do you enjoy newness, risk and adventure? Do you prefer to take things slowly and stay in your comfort zones? Relating to the other sex in a way that acknowledges how God created you is tricky work. Your strengths might indicate that you would relate best one way, but your weaknesses might make that one way hazardous.

We can save ourselves a lot of pain by knowing not only who God has created us to be but how he is still growing us. As a senior in high school I was introverted, commitment-oriented, loyal, emotional and enjoyed relating one-on-one. I wanted to find one person to pour myself into with reckless abandon. I did so. By the end of my freshman year in college I was outgoing, group-oriented, present-minded and rational. I wanted to be in a community and shield my personal life. I did so. By the end of my senior year in college I was a commitment-oriented, loyal, one-on-one, independent, shy people person. Pretty weird, huh?

Our relational desires and needs will change according to our context (remember, there are five factors shaping our way of relating), so we ought not expect to relate to the other sex the same way in every setting. Another variable is the other person; each participant has been made and is being remade by God, and how we relate to one another must take that fact into account.

Listening to Your Conscience

"The Spirit searches everything, even the depths of God. For what human being knows what is truly human except the human spirit that is within? So also no one comprehends what is truly God's except the Spirit of God. Now we have received not the spirit of the world, but the Spirit that is from God, so that we may understand the gifts bestowed on us by God" (1 Corinthians 2:10-12). We have God's Spirit within us: our conscience. If we could only squeegee the fog of selfishness and perverted desire off our conscience, we could make the right decisions all the time.

As we relate to the other sex we need to ask ourselves, "Am I accustomed to listening to my conscience?" Some people seem to have more natural ability to hear their conscience speak, but each of us has the Spirit of God straining to speak to us, regardless of how much we must strain to hear. Be careful not to out step your conscience's vocal range when you are relating to the other sex.

The Bible is our ultimate guideline. Who God is forming us to be dictates our needs and desires in relating to others. Our conscience helps us discover what God wants for us from the wild fray of relationships. Our culture also affects our way of relating, and we must take it into account.

Relating Where You Are

God is the author of and thus the first voice for our lives. He calls us to listen to his voice through prayer, Scripture and our conscience. Other voices call out to us, and we can receive God's wisdom from the people closest to us as well as people not so close to us (even authors!). Our friends and family, our parents or guardians, are invested in us and have knowledge of us that can shed light on who we are, what God has for us and how we might best relate to others. But even in an ideal world of perfect relationships, our cultural surroundings should be woven into, rather than wrapped around, our thoughts and prayers.

Some people have inherited from their family, peers or Christian community one option for relating to the other sex. Some traditions or subcultures claim to have the skinny on the only morally or biblically sound approach to such relationships. But each of us is unique; how could anyone claim that a single way of relating will benefit all people maximally when everyone has such different needs and gifts? We need to weave into the insights of our culture the things we have learned about ourselves, our God and our conscience.

Chapter Ten

Common Connections with the Other Sex

Dating, courtship, community-based relating and shared experience make up the predominant methods of interacting with the other sex. There are others (including cyber-relating), but most people form their relationships with these four models underlying their thinking.

Our Definitions

Dating. A form of relating based mostly on formal shared experiences. The relationship may or may not be initiated by a formal invitation, but it is nurtured and developed intentionally through mostly planned meeting times.

Courtship. A form of relating based on a pre-established formal code or outline. Courtship often involves family members and close friends; its desired end is never short of marriage.

Community-based relating. A form of relating that develops largely within the give-and-take of a larger group of friends. Shared experiences take place primarily within a community context. Many times (though not necessarily) a relationship will begin this way and move into a different form.

Shared experience. Any relationship that develops outside of community, dating or courtship. The beginning of such a relationship could be as simple as working together or sitting next to each other in class.

Some people feel pressure from family to avoid relating to the other sex until they are prepared to marry. Others find themselves set up with someone of the other sex by mutual friends. Still others pair up with someone of the other sex simply to fit in at activities with couple-friends. The common risk of these experiences is to yield to these pressures without considering God's Word, his Holy Spirit and his creative work in us. When we think holistically, we can each create our own combination of these options to achieve our relating potential.

The following scenarios will give you some ideas about how you can find what works best for you.

Anna

Anna is shy, conservative and loyal, devout In her walk with God and eager to hear his voice. She enjoys being in small groups of people and shows her deeper self to a few close friends. When she is able to relax around a group of people, she laughs continually and lights up everyone around her. She likes to think through her decisions of the heart, but she is strongly controlled by her emotions. Her shyness and her faith rarely let her step over the boundaries in relationships, but she cannot deny that she's a romantic. How might Anna relate to the other sex?

Anna relates in one-on-one situations only with close friends, so dating would probably not be the best. She shines in small groups, so community-based relating may be an option. At the same time, she relates most deeply in one-on-one situations when she knows the person well. She is loyal and conservative. A community-based relationship may give way to courting when the time is right.

Jennifer

Jennifer is a social butterfly. Like anyone she needs her time alone, but before long she craves social interaction. She loves to sit in coffee shops and talk, but she also loves sitting in a theater and simply sharing company with friends. She has a hard time sharing intimately and commonly uses humor to avoid potentially deep situations. She is not alone with one person very often and is not very comfortable in such situations. She has also struggled with her relationship with God lately. It is strong for a while and then lacking. She realizes the things about herself she desires to change, but she cannot find the discipline or desire to change them. She clings boldly to rationality, but she is hopelessly romantic, and when the rubber hits the road she listens to her heart. How might Jennifer relate to the other sex?

Jennifer loves groups of people, but she never gets very deep in groups. Community relating might work, but something else would be needed to crack through her shell. She is unbalanced and unpredictable spiritually and emotionally, so a dating relationship could be risky, because her heart could override her conscience and what she knows about God's Word. Courting would most likely be a waste of time without finding some way to relate to people using her strengths and desires first. She enjoys people and activity. She may relate best through community and then through shared experience with one person or a few people outside of the larger community. After she learns to share more deeply, she may continue to relate through shared experience; her expansive and fun-loving personality may not fit well in a courtship. Double or group dating combined with less formal one-on-one relating may work the best for her.

Jack

Jack is outgoing and intense. He loves meeting new people, but he doesn't have much use for large groups. He prefers to find quality conversation in small groups or one on one. Most people genuinely enjoy being with him; he is a great talker, but he is also a great listener. He is highly committed to his best friends, who may be male or female. He is strict in his moral beliefs and highly rational in most situations. He was raised by Christian standards and he believes wholeheartedly in God, but he has little time or need for much of a personal walk with God. He very much likes to be in control of his life and his relationships with the opposite sex. He is very slow to open his heart to people, because his mind does not trust his heart. He prefers not to leave much of anything to chance, so he plans his time and his relationships in advance. How might Jack relate to the other sex?

Jack has had close relationships with women already, but because of his demand for control they were limited in their effect on him. He is not walking with God, so his motives are more likely to be selfish. This makes any form of relating difficult. What is his best hope for getting beyond his barriers so that he can relate? First of all, he needs community to jump-start his faith and challenge him in his selfishness. This community may take the form of a best friend who is right with God, since Jack has little use for larger groups. He is skilled in relating one on one, and he operates by strict moral disciplines. Dating or courting would suit these character traits best. But because of his strict disciplines he might see no need for courtship. Shared experiences and dating would allow more freedom for his one-on-one relating skills to advance the relationship.

All relationships have the capacity to fail if they push beyond healthy limits: the commitment level involved, biblical standards, the boundaries of conscience or the constraints of the surrounding culture. Relationships with the other sex put a lot on the line, but this is not sufficient reason to avoid or neglect them. If any relationship promises more than can be fulfilled, then the relationship will end in heartbreak—heartbreak that must either gradually heal through resolution of the relationship, or scar over and do long-term damage.

Blood, Sweat & Tears: The Aches of Swinging

I have often heard the statement "Dating is practice for failure and breakup." This could be true; all relationships are practice for failure if they push beyond their healthy limits. If we find ourselves in a relationship in which more is being promised than can be fulfilled, then the relationship will be broken. By broken relationship I mean a relationship that has not been given the chance to heal. It has been completely cut off, and the two people involved can no longer communicate. And without resolution, the relationship will leave a scar. A broken relationship is a failure.

Relationships with the other sex may not always move toward being more intimate. Sometimes they move apart. But as long as the relationship is not broken, even in the backing away, then the relationship is not a failure. I have had close relationships with people I never see or talk to anymore. Some of them live two thousand miles away. Some of them are married, in the thick of a new life that is further than two thousand miles from where I am. But we still love and care for each other. We respect each other and remember the closeness of our history. For all practical purposes our relationship started to end when we reached the end of our commitment to each other. But though these relationships are ended, they are not broken; they are not failures.

Relating with the other sex risks much, but this does not mean we should not make the effort. Heartache and joy are both potential outcomes, and each brings wisdom with it. All of us have different tolerance levels for pain and hurt and even joy. So swing freely, but swing with care.

What Can You Honestly Invest? What Is Dishonest?
Have you ever received an overdraft notice in the mail or seen the words "insufficient funds" flash across the screen of an ATM? If we are to avoid falling off the financial edge, we need to keep track of the money in our bank accounts. We should also become masters of managing our relational bank accounts—making the most of our resources while keeping a trained eye on the balance.

When we relate to someone of the other sex, we establish an account of our commitment. This account grows as we work hard in the relationship to gain trust and respect and . . . well, commitment. Some people's accounts are larger than others, but each of us has our own account to work with. So far, so good.

But each of us also deals in the currency of passion. When we are out there working our moves, throwing passion around like it grows on trees, we risk an overdraft in our commitment account. We need to know that our commitment reserves can support our passion expenses before we make a move with the other sex, or we risk dropping into the red zone: relational dishonesty.

All our hard work and spiritual training, all our desire to know God and God's beauty is put to the test at this moment. The music is in full swing, this man or this woman filling a moment with eternity, as far as we can see. Because doling out passion is so thrilling, self-control is our sole means of protecting ourselves from relational disaster. We must earn commitment before passion tries to cash it in.

We can invest honestly in a relationship only the amount that we can back up with commitment. If you cannot commit to the level of intimacy you are sharing, then you are committing relational fraud. You are making promises that most likely will be broken, which can only lead to relational bankruptcy—heartbreak. Nobody gets what was coming to them in a bankruptcy; everybody loses.

There is a difference between heartbreak and heartache. We cannot avoid heart*ache* by being honest. Heartache is part of swinging, part of living life to the full. God never promised us a life free of hurt. Heart*break*, however, is a consequence of sin, hurt that we inflict on one another by promising more than we can deliver. Honesty in relationships, with all the heartache it entails, is a safeguard against heartbreak, a more enduring and devastating hurt.

We need to recognize our intentions and communicate them in all of our relationships. If we are honest in what we promise to another person, but they hear something different, then nothing has been gained. Both people in a relationship must understand and agree on the level of commitment or heartbreak has not been averted.

An Aside
Twitterpation

Ah, twitterpation: that state of ephemeral bliss we all have such an awkward relationship with. You might think that all this practical and rational insight to the other sex is as useful as a tennis racket for straining spaghetti. In the real world there is this thing called twitterpation, and it doesn't play nice with the brain.

We have probably all committed strange and irrational acts due to this unpredictable force, these raging hormones and racing pulses. How can we be intentional about relating to the other sex with all this twittering going on?

Twitterpation is an emotional and biological phenomenon that throughout history has bewildered us. But twitterpation is part of God's plan, and it can be useful in relating to the other sex. Without twitterpation we might never listen to someone's stories about middle school dances and getting braces and burying childhood pets. We might never care about another person enough to eagerly listen to eighteen years of backlogged life. Twitterpation can be the force that draws relatively new acquaintances into deep friendship. Twitterpation is good. But twitterpation is not completely reliable. So how do we make sure that twitterpation is beneficial?

Be aware of twitterpation. It is not evil or shameful; do not hide it or suffocate it. Let other people know when you are twitterpated. A friend called me, waking me from deep sleep, to tell me that she was twitterpated over some guy, and she knew that he was twitterpated over her. She asked me to be an unbiased and rational perspective on their relationship. I was more than glad to do this, and was excited that she trusted me—so excited that I decided to add her story to this book, so you could celebrate her twitterpation with me.

Anyway, the best way to deal with twitterpation is to enjoy it! Let trusted friends keep a less twitterpated eye on you; they may not always tell you what you want to hear, but if you trust them and can listen to what they have to say, then when the time is right your twitterpation will be cause for celebration.

Chapter Eleven

A Glimpse of God's Perfect Beauty

Jesus! If you cannot get excited about embracing God's beauty in your created being when you think of that name, then you need to get to know Jesus better. God's perfect beauty has not existed on earth since Eden, except in the person of Jesus. Who is Jesus? What do we know about the guy to whom God said, "You are my Son, the Beloved; with you I am well pleased" (Luke 3:22)?

Jesus was not a particularly striking man. Physically he was common, like the rest of us. He was not highly educated or uneducated. He was not a rich man or a beggar. From Jesus we can quickly learn much about what God's perfect beauty does not depend on, but then what *does* define God's beauty? What does *pure* mean?

Through the Eyes of Jesus: A Story from John 3:1-21

There before me, standing slightly slouched in the doorway, was a timid figure. The pale moonlight behind him created a paper doll effect with the outlines of his clothing. I had been in conversation with my Father and was expecting a visitor. I had reached for a jar and a wick before I heard the knock. Before I lit the lamp I recognized the man as being a Pharisee, a man by the name of Nicodemus. "Come in, Nicodemus." I placed the jar of flickering yellow flame on a wooden table. Nicodemus jerked slightly and entered the humble residence.

"Thank you, Rabbi. I'm sorry to call so late."

He was an honest man, a lonely man. His intelligence kept him lonely. His lack of answers kept him honest. These things also kept him timid and unsure, qualities that set him apart from his Pharisee brothers who appeared confident but inwardly scurried like field mice under a hawk's shadow.

"Rabbi," Nicodemus spit out suddenly, "we know that you are a teacher who has come from God; for no one can do these signs that you do apart from the presence of God."

He was almost overcome with fear for what I would respond. "Come, sit down. Please." He sat, each of us on opposite sides of the candle. He spoke using the word *we* as if to hide his aloneness and vulnerability. I knew that he held thoughts different from his brothers, thoughts that made him even more alone. Only the peace and security he had long sought would cure his loneliness. "Very truly, I tell you, no one can see the kingdom of God without being born from above."

With that he furrowed his eyebrows, staring momentarily at the table. "How can anyone be born after having grown old? Can one enter a second time into the mother's womb and be born?"

Almost comical. If it were not for his pain I would have laughed. Nicodemus was caught up in a world of rhetoric. I gently tried to steer him clear of his own tangling intellect. "Very truly, I tell you, no one can enter the kingdom of God without being born of water and Spirit. What is born of the flesh is flesh, and what is born of the Spirit is spirit." He was still uncertain and ready to object. I continued. "Do not be astonished that I said to you, 'You must be born from above.' The wind blows where it chooses, and you hear the sound of it, but you do not know where it comes from or where it goes. So it is with everyone who is born of the Spirit."

He wanted to understand so badly, but his hardheaded pride and human intelligence would not let him. "How can these things be?" He cried out the words in a whining voice.

I wanted to cry in response. "You are a teacher of Israel, and yet you do not understand these things? Very truly, I tell you, we speak of what we know and testify to what we have seen; yet you do not receive our testimony. If I have told you about earthly things and you do not believe, how can you believe if I tell you about heavenly things?" Again I paused to give him time to think. I knew that he would not respond at this point. I had intentionally left him with no room to wander. He needed to be so lost that he had no choice but to abandon his logic and accept my truth on faith.

Slowly I lifted his chin with my words. "No one has ascended into heaven except the one who descended from heaven, the Son of Man. And just as Moses lifted up the serpent in the wilderness, so must the Son of Man be lifted up, that whoever believes in him may have eternal life." Come on, Nicodemus. I am enough for you. Let go of your own contempt and believe.

Now was the time to wrap it all up for him—to offer all of life's answers in as simple a package possible for this man who craved complexity. "For God so loved the world that he gave his only Son, so that everyone who believes in him may not perish but may have eternal life. Indeed, God did not send the Son into the world to condemn the world, but in order that the world might be saved through him. Those who believe in him are not condemned; but those who do not believe are condemned already because they have not believed in the name of the only Son of God."

Now his gaze was quite troubled. I felt his sorrow. He feared the judgment of which I spoke. As his thoughts swirled, his stare was drawn to the candle on the table, and I knew how to convey hope to this man—hope enough to continue to seek me, hope enough not to despair. "And this is the judgment, that the light has come into the world, and people loved darkness rather than light because their deeds were evil. For all who do evil hate the light and do not come to the light, so that their deeds may not be exposed. But those who do what is true come to the light, so that it may be clearly seen that their deeds have been done in God."

He continued staring at the tiny flame for a long moment. Then he began to nod his head. At some elementary level, he understood. Even now he was being drawn to the light. I knew that my Father had given him to me to shepherd.

Repeating

I.

I have nights of being a janitor
in one of those buildings with
unflexing ribs repeating like support beams in a mine shaft
and clear outer walls like an aquarium.
I remove others' existence,
return formlessness to the cube-sized voids
and with the light switch on my way out,
darkness to the face of the deep.
There is depth in that moment between switches,
for empty has no end, then a flick
and the next switch returns walls.
In my bubble-sized catacomb I can live
when others are dead and die
every morning.

II.

Jesus, did you have nights of being a carpenter?
Back in Nazareth of Galilee
smoothing a plane over wooden beams
and burying your feet in wood chips
desiring a home-cooked meal by your mother
when your brothers were still your family?
Was it the making of men, breaking down desires
and sending them back to the beginning or
was it the dark hour with its endless possibilities or

the starting over and over
that compelled you to die
and live again?

III.

Of being an alcoholic I sometimes fancy,
but mostly when I am driving
and driving is dear to me. Do not dull
my sense of paradox in driving:
my body resting, my body flying—
both I know are true but
they cannot know each other. This
is my time of genius, asking questions
of myself which outside of my car
I cannot answer.

(Jesus, I want to listen to you
but how can I know you have ever wanted
to be someone else, somewhere
other than where you are?)

Sometimes I have unsolicited trips
when that world inside my car keeps on
beyond its utility of transport. This
I reckon is my drink, my spirits.
I beg the highway to change its course,
or the map to lie so I can find
myself hung over somewhere unknown and new.
One state over or a gas tank later
the voice of someone to whom I used to listen
tells me I should go back to where I started,
So I do.

Jesus' Vision

Jesus worked gingerly with Nicodemus's confusion and vulnerability. How many of us would have seen Nicodemus's late night knocking at the door as an intrusion and an annoyance? How many of us would have been defensive and argued apologetics, morality or logic? How many of us would have blanked out on the blunt facts of the gospel? How many of us would have noticed or even cared about Nicodemus's real needs? How many of us would have responded with so much love and attention to a rival or foe?

Jesus had pure vision. He had God's vision. Therefore none of Nicodemus's beauty or the beauty of the moment escaped Jesus. The Bible records numerous examples of Jesus' pure vision in one-on-one encounters with hurting people. When we are able to see through Jesus' eyes with God's vision, we cannot help but recognize all of God's great beauty.

Heart Conditioning: Seeing with the Eyes and the Heart

Jesus' vision went beyond his eyesight. He saw people and the perfect love of God that dwelt in them through the filter of his heart. The eyes do not see properly without a well-conditioned heart.

Jesus' heart was conditioned to see and love people for who they pretended to be, who they really were and who they were meant to be. He recognized people's beauty and their self-destructiveness. He made room in his heart for them. Imagine how many people took up residence in Jesus' heart; how huge it must be! Jesus offered a place of refuge in his huge heart at every encounter. His heart stretched to fit the crowds that pressed in on him for healing.

How important were Jesus' times with his Father! I imagine he cried out the pain of all his broken residents, allowing God to stretch his heart larger to make more room. Stretched to its physical limits, Jesus' heart burst on the cross to flood the world with his healing love.

Jesus taught through his actions that somehow, the eyes must be attached to the heart. God's beauty is on display in every person and can be seen through the eyes of our hearts.

Getting Focused

Jesus fought all of our struggles. He was tempted but never perverted. He doesn't close his eyes to the needs of a messed up culture: hookers, adulterers, CEOs, TV evangelists, murderers, homosexuals—perverts of all stripes. Through the mess he saw the vulnerable faces of his Father's children.

We can focus on Jesus as a model for providing shelter to needy people and recognizing God's beauty in others. But we are not Jesus. We cannot endure every temptation without sinning. We cannot stretch our hearts to shelter everyone and everything we encounter. We must open our hearts with care, and this means focusing *through* Jesus as well.

I grew up on a ranch, and part of growing up on a ranch is learning to shoot wild animals that threatened our livestock and crops, or promised a good dinner. I used a scope to target coyotes or bunnies or other small critters which I probably shouldn't have been shooting. The scope projected four little lines—called crosshairs—extending from its center. The target was the object of my search, but the crosshairs lined up my target so that I could achieve my goal. I had to sight my target without losing the cross image.

The cross image is central to God's beauty. Jesus died on a cross to be our scope and our target—the way, and the truth and the life. To find God's beauty in the midst of the perversion we and others have created, we must look for Christ in the world, looking through Christ's unperverted eyes.

Many books attempt to describe and flesh out what Christ did on the cross. Creeds and doctrines try to express the meaning of Jesus' death. But you do not have to be a Bible scholar to see the world through the cross. You just have to believe that your perversions were nailed there with Christ and are now dead and buried. And you have to believe that the cross is left empty—that Christ rose from the dead and your new life rose with him. [*]

What a great time to be alive. Through Christ we have been given the opportunity to rediscover God's beauty in our lives and in the lives of those around us. Our broken and wounded but restored hearts are the most fertile soil on this earth for the reawakening of God's beauty in and among us.

---

[*]What exactly has Jesus done for us at the cross? If you really want to challenge your mind with this subject read John Stott's *The Cross of Christ* (Downers Grove, Ill.: InterVarsity Press, 1986).

Chapter Twelve

How Do I Do This?

So if purity of the heart comes by seeing God's beauty rather than my perversions and by having God's focus with my heart and eyes, *how do we do this?* There are no easy answers—well, there is an easy answer, but it is not easily done.

Surrender. Give in. Stop trying so hard.

When I was learning how to use a shotgun, my father took me out behind the ranch house to shoot clay pigeons—disks flung at high speeds out of a variety of different gadgets. I loaded my 4x10 gauge, double-barreled shotgun as my father loaded a launcher with a single pigeon. I brought the butt of the gun to my shoulder, flipped off the safety, readied myself and squeaked "Pull."

My father pulled the cord releasing the flying disk into a high arching flight. I squinted my eye and focused intently down the line of the barrel. I tried to follow the arc of the pigeon, but I couldn't move fast enough or hold steady enough. The pigeon died, all right, but from the impact of the hard, dry ground—not from the blast of my tiny 4x10. I never even pulled the trigger. I was about to learn a lesson about shotguns, but I did not know that it would be a life lesson as well.

My father explained gently that shooting at birds was not like plinking at turtles in a pond. I would not have time to aim. There would be no time to calculate once the bird had flown. He told me how to prepare ahead of time.

"Think about the wind, where you will be pointing your barrel, which direction you should turn and the range of your gun." There was work I could do, but I was trying to do it all at the last minute. I wanted to be certain that my effort and skill shattered the clay pigeon.

There's a significant difference between a rifle—which I had used before—and the shotgun I was learning to shoot. A rifle projects a single slug of metal. Thus to hit a target with a rifle requires fine aim. A shotgun, on the other hand, fires anywhere from a few to dozens of round balls of metal, or "shot," which project over a large area. Thus a shotgun does not require fine aim; at least one of these pieces of shot is likely to hit its target.

I needed to look beyond the barrel of the gun, using it only to make sure I was pointed in the right direction. I needed to match the path of the pigeon with the barrel, rather than cross it or contradict it. I needed to lead the pigeon just a little, letting it fly into the shot. I needed to keep the gun from jerking when I pulled the trigger. None of these directions included aim.

I packed all of the information into my head and prepared myself to fire once again. "Pull." The spinning clay flew high and arching again. I tried to match its path, leading it a little. I panicked. I finally pulled the trigger right as the pigeon struck the ground. I shot a bunch of orange buffalo grass.

Without hesitation my father loaded the launcher a third time. "This time, just shoot it. Shoot it as soon as you can."

"Pull." He pulled the cord. I pulled the trigger.

"Good shot." My father said. I watched the clay pigeon still whizzing untouched through the air. But I understood how to use a shotgun. I needed to surrender myself to it.

To surrender does not mean to do nothing. It does not mean giving up. To surrender is to give in, and stop trying too hard. In my life with God surrender has meant thinking about God, the people he has placed around me, the life he has for me, the gifts he has given me. God pulls the cord; I pull the trigger. God controls the pigeon and the shot; as I surrender myself to that fact, I stay on target.

To live God's will in this life we need his divine instinct. We don't need fine aim or detailed instruction, though God sharpens our aim and offers us instruction. We don't even need to always hit our target square on. We do need to pull the trigger. So surrender. Just pull the trigger. Stop aiming. Stop working so hard to take some of the credit. As we spend more time with God, he will sharpen our instincts.

Let Us Sum Up

In our quest for purity and beauty we can have a spectrum of response. On one hand, we could ban all controversial images and experiences from our body, thus forfeiting our right to and our gift of beauty and wonder. On the other hand, we could allow all images and all experiences entrance into our bodies, thus dulling, destroying and confusing their beauty and crushing wonder.

Or we can turn to the Bible and Jesus for wisdom in discerning God's beauty from our perversion. We can focus on God's beauty with our eyes and our hearts. And we can see with our eyes and our hearts God's beauty all around.

A Psalm of Surrender

Dear God,

I find myself in a dark room filled with false promises, pine boxes and deception in flaming brown paper bags. My hands are tied behind my back by my own perversion. Satan has his hand on the light switch and his leg stuck out in my path. I don't know where you are or what beauty looks like. You could place it on my chest and it would only contribute to my suffocation.

God, I want your grace. I want you to forgive me, to save me, to love me. How could I want anything more? Here I am. Consume me. Do I matter?

Send me. Send me anywhere out of this hell. Send me. Push me. Pull me. Throw me. Save me. Kill me. Please do something! Or is Satan your herald—your mouthpiece and errand boy? Is he carrying out your verdict on me?

I'm sorry. God, I am sorry. I'm worthless. I want to trust you. I close my eyes and open my mouth, but I receive nothing—nothing but my own spit and acid upheaved from my stomach. I know I can't do anything to be loved by you. I know I cannot earn your forgiveness. I know that I cannot purify myself. But how can I not try?

How can I not try? I want to be loved. I want to be forgiven. I want to be clean. Do it God, please. Do it now. I cannot last another round. My wounds bleed and hiss— infected, rotting. My eyes wander wildly in my head but cannot see through my swollen flesh. My tongue blocks my throat. All of this I feel with pen and paper as I draw with words my gory, holocaust frame in letters to friends—friends absent, uninterested, unknowing.

Help me! Someone help me.

God, you have separated me. You have taken any comfort I might have had. You have driven me to depend on you. Now where are you? I want you to take over. I need you to stop me—protect me from myself.

I will not struggle to meet you. I am still. I am curled in the corner. I do not move even to combat the mice that gnaw at my skin. I wait for you to pick me up, untie me, clean me, unwrap the gift, open my eyes, feed me, and help me to chew.

Why, God, must it be this way? Why do you serve me? How does my Lord bow lower than I?

How could it be any different? How could I serve you? You could not possibly need my service. You do not. You are too great for me. You need nothing. God, by serving, you are great! God, you are separate from all other gods, because you do not threaten or bribe in order to be served. You do not need people to serve you. No! You require that we let you serve us. In this way, you prove your might. And you prove your point.

You do not need me to do anything, but you have chosen to give me power and choice. I choose to stand. I choose to walk and let you guide my steps.

Forgive me, God, for trying to save face—for trying in some small way to be worthy or worthwhile. Thank you for saving me from myself. Thank you for giving me yourself. Help me to live in your presence, helpless without you, forever.

Write your own psalm of surrender, being as brutally honest as possible.

To God be the glory, forever and ever. Amen.

Epilogue
The Joy & Freedom in Pure Beauty

Purity of heart is not a prerequisite for God's love. As a matter of fact, purity of heart is not possible without God's love. God created pure beauty. He desires to restore us to this pure beauty if we will submit to his care. Psalm 23:2-3 relates this fact:

> He makes me lie down in green pastures;
> he leads me beside still waters;
> he restores my soul.
> He leads me in right paths
> for his name's sake.

Is God to be trusted? If we believe he is, we should turn to him for help rather than reverting to our hollow, sinful patterns. God makes big promises:

> For surely I know the plans I have for you, says the Lord, plans for your welfare and not for harm, to give you a future with hope. Then when you call upon me and come and pray to me, I will hear you. When you search for me, you will find me; if you seek me with all your heart, I will let you find me, says the Lord, and I will restore your fortunes and gather you from all the nations and all the places where I have driven you. (Jeremiah 29:11-14)

Psalm 16:5-11 gives witness to the benefits of trusting God.

> The LORD is my chosen portion and my cup;
>> you hold my lot.
> The boundary lines have fallen for me in pleasant places;
>> I have a goodly heritage.
> I bless the LORD who gives me counsel;
>> in the night also my heart instructs me.
> I keep the LORD always before me;
>> because he is at my right hand, I shall not be moved.
> Therefore my heart is glad, and my soul rejoices;
>> my body also rests secure.
> For you do not give me up to Sheol,
>> or let your faithful one see the Pit.
> You show me the path of life.
>> In your presence there is fulness of joy;
>> in your right hand are pleasures forevermore.

Read those passages carefully because they are full of life. God guides our paths. He has plans for us, plans that benefit us and bring us hope. God will not hide from us. All we have to do is look for him. God will restore us. He will bring us back from the exile of our perversions. The boundaries that God gives us are pleasant and good. God directs us day and night. He protects us. God gives us life. He shows us the way to that life. God offers us a life of complete joy and never-ending pleasures.

The Edge of Light

I.

My life always strikes out at death
like a scared man abandoned on a beach
with only a dying torch to
fight off everything outside, bursting
the bubble of failing light and life:

One lock of curled hair drips
sweat along the bridge of my nose,
My chapped skin is lit and orange-warmed
by tongues of sun and exposed
by a small cotton shirt.

Scurvy gulls hover overhead smearing
the air through their feathers and
swearing shrill and pissed
over their beaks, under their tail, down the beach:
Dig the hole for yourself, skinny kid.

I open a bag of Cheetos
and shake them into the hole,
bury them over with sand,
place the plastic pompously on top,
glare up at the damned birds and skip away.

II.

Light never strikes out at darkness
like a scared man abandoned on a beach
with only a dying torch to
fight off everything outside, bursting
the bubble of failing light and life.

Outside the scared man's shield of protection (and paranoia)
no fangs beg to soften him with poison.
The torch creates what it hides, frenzies
what it fends off. The hissing is only oxygen
and the man's searing lungs in competition with the torch to breathe.

III.

Life lives at the edge of light
like a silent woman waiting,

able to imagine darkness and
able to understand light, to lie with another
and show him God.

She stands wearing cotton summer,
forming yet falling loosely around
and over her hips, stomach and chest
containing transparent heart—latched,
not locked. She sees scared man's black shadow
on the beach, burned out of orange paper by the torch.
He cannot see beyond the flickering light
out to where she stands knee-deep in a hole
filling slowly with sand and foam
as the water rushes and recedes.

IV.

The fire, which bore him into light,
woke him up to life through truth and pain,
and gave him first sight, now burns his skin
until he throws it. Walking around the fire
back off the beach in the dunes
his eyes adjust under the moon to the wave's silver slips
brushing gently open and sliding under the sand,
and Life's soft skin is bright when they lie down together on the edge
of light beneath the wind's gossip and salt
using the darkness to dilate themselves.

He lets the morning minutes swarm
swollen in his throat and heart
and teach his body to float into midday, a cork
and burn in the evening every drop of wine, every second
until he's an empty bottle, purpose filled and unashamed.

Life on the Edge of Light

We should not fear perversion as master of our lives. The world we live in and the people we love are perverted, and they need our love, not our fear. Perversion cannot overtake us. God has promised that. We should not cling tightly to a rigid regimen of rules and a black and white gospel so that the only grace we experience is after we die. We can choose to live our entire life within the light of God's initial gift of eternal life. A single torch with a short life span is all the light we get from life. We can cling to it and be blind to what lies beyond it, thus helping only ourselves (1 Corinthians 3:12-15). Or we can let go of it. We can lay down our lives to serve others. We can lay down the torch to pick up the cross. We can lose our lives in order to gain life.

If you have been to a bonfire, you know that warmth and safety from the unknown elements of the night are found close to the fire. But if you are too near the fire, you cannot see beyond its immediate illumination. You may be safe and warm, but you are blind to the darkness.

Millions of people stumble in that darkness. What on earth shall we do? The only way we can stay warm and safe and yet extend our light to those in the shadows is to live at the edge of the light. It will not be as warm or safe as being right next to the fire; we may need to draw closer from time to time. But people stumbling in the shadows often fear the light as much as those who sit safe and warm fear the shadows. Light is painful and confusing when we are accustomed to the dark; many will not come on their own, but they must come if they would be safe and warm. So we must be on the edge of the light to lead them to safety. God has chosen it to be this way.

The fulfilling life that Jesus talks about is waiting at the edge of the light. When we embrace life at the edge of the light, we will find ourselves purged of our perversions and renewed in the pure beauty of God.

Further Reading

Anderson, Keith R. *Friendships That Run Deep: Seven Ways to Build Lasting Re-lationships.* Downers Grove, Ill.: InterVarsity Press, 1997. This is a must-read for those who have ever wondered what makes a friend a friend. It brings to light the necessary elements of friendship that we overlook, take for granted or are just plain ignorant about.

Arnold, Johann Christoph. *A Plea for Purity.* Farmington, Penn.: Plough, 1996. This book provides a different perspective on the issues in *Tainted Love.* Good reading.

Manning, Brennan. *The Ragamuffin Gospel.* Sisters, Ore.: Multnomah Press, 2000. This book brings God's grace down to earth in refreshing mouthfuls. It is an awesome book for weary and haggard saints who feel that the love of God cannot be for them or need encouragement to live.

Richardson, Rick. *Evangelism Outside the Box.* Downers Grove, Ill.: InterVarsity Press, 2000. This is the only evangelism book I have been able to finish. I include it in this list because it wonderfully portrays how community, friend-ship and witness spawn God's beauty in our lives and the lives of everyone around us.

Saint-Exupéry, Antoine de. *The Little Prince.* London: Harcourt Brace Jovano-vich, 1971. This is one of my favorite books, and I believe it should be read by everyone about once a year. It captures much of the unseen beauty of life and the irony of what we make of it.

Starkey, Mike. *God, Sex & the Search for Lost Wonder.* Downers Grove, Ill.: Inter-Varsity Press, 1998. This is an awesome book for awakening us to the disas-trous results of sin in the realms of sex and beauty. It explains how we have come to where we are and where we can go from here.

Willingham, Russell. *Breaking Free: Understanding Sexual Addiction & the Heal-ing Power of Jesus.* Downers Grove, Ill.: InterVarsity Press, 1999. This is a powerful book on a topic too often shied away from. Read this book. Recom-mend it to your friends. Get together and discuss the topics it brings to the surface.